Internships
In Psychology

Internships
In Psychology

The APAGS Workbook
for Writing Successful Applications
and Finding the Right Match

Edited by

Carol Williams-Nickelson
and Mitchell J. Prinstein

With contributions by

Shane J. Lopez and W. Gregory Keilin

American Psychological Association • Washington, DC

Published by
American Psychological Association
750 First Street, NE
Washington, DC 20002
www.apa.org

To order
APA Order Department
P.O. Box 92984
Washington, DC 20090-2984
Tel: (800) 374-2721; Direct: (202) 336-5510
Fax: (202) 336-5502; TDD/TTY: (202) 336-6123
Online: www.apa.org/books/
E-mail: order@apa.org

In the U.K., Europe, Africa, and the Middle East, copies may be ordered from
American Psychological Association
3 Henrietta Street
Covent Garden, London
WC2E 8LU England

Typeset in Trump Medieval by World Composition Services, Inc., Sterling, VA

Printer: Phoenix Color Corp., Hagerstown, MD
Cover Designer: Naylor Design, Washington, DC
Technical/Production Editors: Dan Brachtesende and Emily Leonard

The opinions and statements published are the responsibility of the authors, and such opinions and statements do not necessarily represent the policies of the American Psychological Association.

Printed in the United States of America

CONTENTS

FOREWORD

Nadine J. Kaslow

It is an honor and a pleasure to write a foreword for *Internships in Psychology: The APAGS Workbook for Writing Successful Applications and Finding the Right Match*. Internship is often one of the most exciting and stimulating aspects of students' graduate education in psychology. However, the internship application process can be challenging. This workbook provides a thorough, useful, and up-to-date toolkit for intern applicants.

The editors have included all of the essential information needed for successful application to internship. Readers will find this workbook to be an invaluable guide, and I encourage you to consult it often. Please remember that your best application will be one in which you build on the prior experiences of others while communicating who you are both personally and professionally.

I commend Carol Williams-Nickelson, PsyD; Mitch Prinstein, PhD; Shane Lopez, PhD; and Greg Keilin, PhD, for their outstanding contributions. This workbook is a "must have" for all intern applicants.

Best wishes to all of you who are applying to internship.

PREFACE

Once upon a time, there were no helpful resources available to help students navigate the internship application process. But there was a lot of anxiety, confusion, and many questions that led each of us to become involved with local and national associations that advocate for students and attend to training issues. We served on committees, were elected to offices, and were asked to speak at conferences about the internship process, ultimately leading to the creation of the first American Psychological Association of Graduate Students (APAGS) Special Preconvention Workshop on the Internship Application Process, which was presented at the 2000 Annual Convention of the American Psychological Association (APA) in Washington, DC.

We created a set of handouts for the workshop, which we conceived as a workbook that would help applicants review each aspect of the internship application process in a careful, systematic manner. We hoped that, through the workshop and the workbook, we would help students reconsider the internship application process as an opportunity to consult with advisors, develop professional goals, meet dozens of professionals with a range of experiences, and find an opportunity to discuss their professional development and interests with people outside of their graduate program. By reframing the tasks involved in this process, the application procedure might seem a little less cumbersome, and applicants could focus on finding not just a match but finding the *right* match for them.

The workshop was a hit, and so was the workbook! We received extraordinary feedback and numerous requests for additional copies of the workbook during the year. Rather than asking students to wait an entire year (until the next preconvention workshop) before they could obtain a copy, APAGS decided to make the workbook available between conventions. Over time, the book evolved into a more thoroughly developed formal document that became a valuable resource, even for those unable to attend the workshop. After its fifth revised edition and the shipment of nearly 4,000 requested copies to internship applicants between 2000 and 2003, APA Books proposed publishing the workbook for broader distribution. We were pleased that the workbook would be made available to a greater number of students and that they shared our goal of keeping the price of the workbook low to accommodate students' limited budgets. A portion of the proceeds from this book has been directed to the APAGS committee to continue supporting programs that will directly benefit students. In addition, the editors and contributors will receive no direct financial gain from their work on this project.

We have organized this volume to remain practically oriented and include a discussion of each aspect of the internship process. As in the former editions, we have included numerous examples to help applicants calculate their clinical hours, compose essays, draft thank you notes, and practice interview questions. The examples are from real applicants, all of whom successfully obtained an internship match; they are neither ideal nor flawless but are realistic, excellent examples that illustrate many of the suggestions offered in this volume. We are grateful to the brave internship applicants who provided us with their materials to present anonymously in this book.

This volume also has some new features, including relevant updates regarding the Association of Psychology Postdoctoral and Internship Centers (APPIC) Uniform Application for Psychology Internships, the computer match system, and the most recent data regarding placement rates. We have also added a section of frequently asked questions that were raised regularly during the workshop.

We hope this volume will provide readers with the support and assistance they need to successfully navigate the internship application process. This resource is just one of several services provided for students by APAGS, a group within APA committed to representing, leading, advocating, and developing resources for graduate psychology students. APAGS and APPIC have developed and continue to cultivate a close relationship so that APAGS can inform APPIC of the needs, concerns, successes, and ideas of internship applicants and that APPIC can advise APAGS of new programs, improved systems, and other information that is useful for APAGS members negotiating the internship process.

Good luck to you all!

ACKNOWLEDGMENTS

Thanks to you, intern applicants! This workbook was developed to address your needs and was shaped by your feedback and encouragement during our annual American Psychological Association of Graduate Students (APAGS) Internship Workshop. Your ongoing support and expression of gratitude has been our inspiration and motivating force to complete this project. Your participation in APAGS has also helped to make our workshop and workbook available to students each year. We hope this book offers you some direction, comfort, and a little humor throughout the internship application process.

We also thank all of the students who voluntarily provided sections of their actual internship application materials for use in this workbook, without any expectation of recognition or reward. Their gesture of goodwill and camaraderie is greatly appreciated by APAGS, because their work will help future generations of internship applicants.

We also gratefully acknowledge Richard Suinn, PhD, past president of the American Psychological Association (APA), and the APA Board of Directors for allocating seed money from their limited contingency funds in 2000 to help launch the workshop and workbook in an effort to make available quality internship resources and training materials. The continued support of Nadine J. Kaslow, PhD, past chair of the Association of Psychology Postdoctoral and Internship Centers (APPIC), and the entire APPIC Board is deserving of tremendous recognition for their dedication to students and to internship training.

Our contributors, long-time collaborators, and good friends, W. Gregory Keilin, PhD, and Shane J. Lopez, PhD, deserve more than thanks for their ongoing efforts, their commitment to students, and their support. Both Shane and Greg have been extraordinary leaders in their work on student training issues, particularly in their national service dedicated toward internship supply and demand, match, and issues with the APPIC Uniform Application for Psychology Internships.

Carol Williams-Nickelson would like to thank the staff of the University of Notre Dame Counseling Center, especially Sue Steibe-Pasalich, PhD; Patrick Utz, PhD; Micky Franco, PhD; Rita Donley, PhD; and Dominic Vachon, PhD, for a memorable and richly rewarding internship experience. The immeasurable support provided by her husband David Nickelson, PsyD, JD, and her colleagues at APA, particularly L. Michael Honaker, PhD, her supervisor and APA chief operating officer and deputy chief executive officer, is deeply appreciated.

Mitch Prinstein extends unending gratitude to his mentors, Annette La Greca, PhD, and Tony Spirito, PhD, for their career guidance and support, as well as to Audrey Zakriski, PhD; Greta Francis, PhD; Fran D'Elia, PhD; Rod Gragg, PhD; and Donn Posner, PhD, for an excellent internship experience. Mitch also extends thanks to his friends and family for everything, always.

Internships
In Psychology

1 GETTING STARTED: GENERAL OVERVIEW OF THE INTERNSHIP APPLICATION PROCESS

Carol Williams-Nickelson and W. Gregory Keilin

The psychology internship application process can be a simultaneously rewarding, exhausting, stressful, and exciting process. Your internship training marks the beginning of the final stages of your graduate career in professional psychology and is a milestone that you should be proud of reaching. Congratulations!

You have been preparing for internship since your first day of graduate school. As a result, you have acquired many valuable experiences that can make you very attractive to the right internship program. The process of gathering materials, calculating your clinical hours, developing your curriculum vitae (CV), establishing and articulating your internship and career goals, interviewing with various internship sites, and finally being matched and going on internship is one of the most valuable exercises you will undertake as a graduate student. This process will help you review and assess all of your previous training, evaluate your collective graduate experiences, define your training and career goals, practice your job application and interviewing skills, and launch you into professional status as a practitioner.

This chapter provides you with a broad overview of the entire internship application process and gives you some organizational tools to assist you in preparation. It is no secret that decisions about internship are often difficult and anxiety provoking. The process includes many unknown factors that you may be contemplating: "Where will I go? Will I measure up? Will my application be competitive? Do I really have what it takes to make it? Can I move? Will I survive living in a region that has snow? Will my family be supportive? How will I live on the small stipend I am paid? What will my supervisors be like? Will I connect with my fellow interns? What will be next for me after internship? Will I have a positive experience?" As you well know, change is rarely easy and almost always stressful. We hope to help you eliminate some of the unproductive worry you may be experiencing and instead capitalize on the normal, productive, and motivating anxiety that is a natural part of doing anything new and different, particularly when you are being evaluated.

This chapter offers practical guidance for preparing your application and getting ready for interviews. It can help you put things in perspective. We understand that you may be worried about the many nuances of where and how to apply for internship and especially how to present yourself to an entirely new group of faculty and supervisors who will be evaluating you all over again. After all, you have probably already established yourself in your program as a competent student with a variety of talents. Now you are tasked with marketing and demonstrating your competence and talents to a new group of evaluators. This is not the first time that you will have to do this, nor will it be the last. Each time you apply for a new job, even if you have a stellar and well-known reputation, you will have to sell yourself and your skills. Preparing for and applying to internships is one of the best, most comprehensive, ways of practicing your marketing strategy for future jobs and opportunities. Do it well this time, and you will gain valuable knowledge about yourself that will benefit you for years to come.

This chapter discusses four areas to help you survey and prepare for what is ahead of you in the application process. First, we review internship application milestones, those that mark the major tasks in the process and help you track your overall progress. We present a sequential checklist that details the major preparatory work you will need to begin now to ensure that you will have an easy time completing your Association of Psychology Postdoctoral and Internship Centers (APPIC) Application for Psychology Internships (the AAPI). We review the *APPIC Directory Online* and discuss developing your strategy for the number of sites and geographic regions to apply to. We present statistics from previous years about the number of sites students have applied to and their match rates. Finally, we discuss your psychological approach to the process and how you can prepare yourself to be open-minded about this next level of your training. So, relax as much as you can, and do your best to learn from and enjoy this process.

INTERNSHIP MILESTONES

The internship application process can be long and arduous. Consider the process to be a series of small manageable tasks. To help you review these tasks and ensure that you have missed none, consult the "Internship Milestones at a Glance" checklist (see Exhibit 1.1) throughout the application process. We encourage you to refer to this list often and record the dates that you accomplish each milestone.

The more organized you are, the easier it will be to complete the AAPI and meet the many overlapping deadlines that extend over several weeks. The suggested checklist can help you arrange all of your supporting application materials so that, when it is time, you can complete your AAPI with minimal frustration and scrambling for information. Obtaining and organizing the information you will need to report on the AAPI can be a long process, so you need to get started early.

Step 1. Visit the APPIC Web Site

You may want to begin the internship application process with a visit to the APPIC Web site. APPIC was founded in 1968 and has a membership of nearly 700 internship and postdoctoral programs across the United States and Canada. APPIC oversees the internship selection process and provides several services to make the process easier for students, such as the APPIC Match and Clearinghouse, a directory that is available in online and printed versions, a standardized internship application, and resources

Exhibit 1.1. *Internship Milestones at a Glance*

Date Completed

1. Compute practica hours, including anticipated hours. _____
2. Download the latest version of the APPIC Application for Psychology Internships (AAPI) from http://www.appic.org. _____
3. Use the APPIC Directory to find sites that match your interests. Review each site's Web-based materials, or request their materials via e-mail or regular mail. _____
4. Register for the Match (see the APPIC Web site). _____
5. Prepare curriculum vitae. _____
6. Request letters of recommendation. _____
7. Draft application essays. _____
8. Complete the AAPI (and any supplemental materials that may be site specific) and write individualized cover letters. _____

RELAX AND WAIT

9. Begin to schedule interviews. _____
10. Practice a sample case presentation. _____
11. Review materials for each site, and decide if you would like to complete a literature search on some of the people you will interview with (if appropriate). _____
12. Compose your questions for internship sites. _____
13. Send thank-you notes/follow-up letters (optional). _____
14. Submit rank order for the Match before the deadline. _____

for students and programs to resolve problems and difficulties encountered during the selection process.

Although APPIC is not an accrediting agency, its members are required to meet certain criteria to be accepted for membership. Nearly all of the more than 450 internship sites accredited by the American Psychological Association (APA) and the Canadian Psychological Association are members of APPIC, and an additional 150 nonaccredited programs are members as well.

You will need to visit three parts of the APPIC Web site (www.appic.org):

1a. *The AAPI.* Download the most recent AAPI, and be sure you are using the version applicable to your application year.
1b. *The Directory.* Most students find that the APPIC Directory is their most useful source of information on internship programs, as it lists the more than 600 programs that are current APPIC members. The APPIC Directory is available in two forms: a printed version and an online version. All internship applicants are required to pay a fee for use of the online version at the time of registration for the Match; however, applicants do not have to wait until this fee is paid to use the directory, as it is publicly available for searching at any time. Entering a set of search parameters and clicking the "Search" button will yield a list of internship programs that match your criteria. You may then click on any internship program in that list to display more information about that specific program.
1c. *The MATCH-NEWS E-Mail List.* This provides news, tips, and information from APPIC about the selection process and the Match.

Here are some tips on getting the most out of searching the *APPIC Directory Online:*

- You may specify as many or as few search parameters as you wish. Increasing the number of search parameters used generally decreases the number of internship programs returned by the search.
- You may find it useful to search for internships that accept applicants from your specific type of graduate program (e.g., school psychology, EdD programs).
- If you are looking for part-time, 2-year internships, use the "Part-Time" search option to locate such programs.
- You can search for any of the 60 "Training Opportunities" listed. For example, you could search for all programs that serve a Spanish-speaking population, conduct cognitive rehabilitation, or specialize in child neuropsychology.
- You will find that each program's listing includes directions on how to obtain additional information about the program and its application requirements (most programs have either a Web site or a printed brochure available).

Most applicants do not need to buy the printed version of the directory, as the online version is more than enough to meet their needs. In addition, most doctoral programs purchase a copy of the printed directory for use by their students. However, if you do wish to obtain a copy of the printed version, it may be purchased through the APPIC Central Office.

In addition to the APPIC Directory, faculty members and fellow graduate students are often excellent sources of information about internships. Contacting students from your program who are currently on internship or who have recently completed an internship may allow you to benefit from their internship search experiences. In addition, faculty will often know of internship programs that have had positive experiences with other students from your program and thus may be particularly welcoming of your application.

For students who are looking for internships in California, the California Psychology Internship Council (see www.capic.net) publishes a directory of internship programs in that state. Many of these programs are not APA-accredited nor are members of APPIC, and most do not participate in the APPIC Match. In addition, many of the positions at these sites are filled by students who are enrolled in doctoral programs in California.

Step 2. Decide Which Sites You Will Be Applying To

Once you have reviewed the information on the APPIC Directory, you should obtain as much material as possible about each site you are interested in. For many sites, you may download brochures, descriptions, and applications. For others, a simple postcard, letter, or e-mail will be sufficient to request application materials.

Review each site to determine the potential match. This will be difficult, as many sites sound quite similar on paper. It may be helpful to review each site with your specific goals in mind (see chapter 3 for a discussion on constructing goals for internship training). Also be sure to discuss your decisions with colleagues, your director of

Table 1.1. *Internship Applicants Who Successfully Matched, Based on the Number of Submitted Applications*

No. of Applications	% Matched in 2004
1–5	77
6–10	86
11–15	91
16–20	86
21 or more	93

Note. Data from the 2004 Post-Match Internship Survey.

clinical training, and former students from your program who have recently completed the application process.

How many sites should you apply to? Each year, many applicants wonder how many internship programs they should apply to in order to maximize their chances of being placed. APPIC's most recent study on this issue was conducted in 2004, where 1,515 applicants (47% of all registered) completed a post-Match survey.

In 2004, applicants reported submitting an average of 12.4 applications (mean = 12, mode = 12). See Table 1.1 for a summary of how well applicants did in the Match based on the number of applications submitted. Here is what we recommend:

- Most internship applicants will best be served by applying to between 10 and 15 internship sites. Applying to more than 15 does not appear to improve the chances of being matched; in fact, it can result in more interviews than an applicant can reasonably participate in (based on time, travel, and financial limitations).
- Do not apply to all highly competitive sites, as doing so could significantly reduce your chances of being matched.
- If you are geographically restricted or need to attend a part-time internship, you might find your options to be limited. Applicants who are interested in part-time options may wish to contact programs that do not offer a part-time option to see if they will consider offering one.

Step 3. Get Organized

Once you have chosen the sites to which you will apply, it behooves you to organize your materials, note your deadlines, and start collecting the information you will need to complete the application phases of the process. Here are some important suggestions:

- Pay attention to and record the application deadlines for every site you download or request information from. Application deadlines vary, and if you are not careful, you can miss some deadlines while you are waiting to receive each site's information.
- Complete cover sheets to attach to site information that you have gathered that includes basic information about each site you are considering (see Exhibit 1.2 for an example).

Exhibit 1.2. *Application Site Requirements Sample Cover Sheet*

Application Requirements

Date Due: _____

Interest: High   Medium   Low

Site: _____

Materials Needed	Due	✔
Notes:		

- Once site information and application materials are all collected, order the application packets with cover sheets from highest to lowest interest, factoring in first and last application deadlines. Use this organizational mechanism to decide how many and to which sites you want to apply.
- Review your site interests and preferences with your mentor or a trusted faculty member for their input and impressions.
- Begin gathering and organizing all of the information that you will need to report on the AAPI.
- Obtain the information (i.e., costs) and the required forms for ordering transcripts—from both undergraduate and graduate institutions.
- Know your undergraduate, master's, and doctoral grade point averages.
- Identify four people whom you would like to ask to write your recommendation letters. Three letters are usually required by each site, but it may be good to have one extra for backup. However, avoid having more than four letters sent.

- Make an appointment with and begin talking to the four potential references, so they can get to know you and your interests and talents to write a strong letter.
- Provide your references with a copy of your CV, essays, goals for internship, and other important information that will make their letter writing as easy as possible. Do not wait until the last minute to do this, and do not do this too far in advance—to prevent a rush job or a forgotten job. Ask your references if they would like you to provide them with stamped envelopes addressed to the internship sites where you want the letters sent. Some references prefer to send their letters on their own letterhead envelopes. Others appreciate the ease of having prepared envelopes.
- Begin collecting the materials necessary to complete your CV (e.g., dates of training, clinical supervisors' names, titles and authors for presentations or publications).
- Organize, review, and begin tallying your clinical hours and testing experience (see chapter 2 for more information on the AAPI).

Step 4. Develop a Helpful Mindset

As we have informally talked with, advised, and consoled students preparing for internship, four applicant mindsets have consistently emerged as common psychological approaches to the internship process. Some people may consider these as stress management strategies, coping processes, defense mechanisms, heuristics, unconscious slips, or socially constructed narratives. Whatever you choose to call them, you will undoubtedly identify with some of these cognitions and perhaps even notice them in your peers.

The following taxonomy of themes seems to capture the beliefs of most students preparing to apply for internship. As you review them, see if your thinking matches any of these common beliefs and, if so, whether you are comfortable with your approach or if you would like to make some cognitive shifts.

The "Just do it!" mindset. This mindset is characterized by one or more of the following thoughts and beliefs:

- "Internship is just another hoop that I have to jump through to get my degree and get on with my life."
- "Internship isn't that important in the grand scheme of things, anyway."
- "I'll just do it and get it over with in the most painless way possible."
- "I'll take anything, anywhere, whatever I can get—because I can endure anything for one year."

The "I'm too prepared and talented for them" mindset. This approach is characterized by one or more of the following thoughts and beliefs:

- "My practicum experiences were outstanding—probably the best in the country. I deserve to be a psychologist *now*. I don't want or need to do an internship."
- "My program was so fabulous; there couldn't possibly be anything else an internship site can teach me."

- "This is one of those easy sites. This year will be a breeze."
- "I'm smarter than most of the internship faculty at this site!"

The "This decision will determine my life course" mindset. This mindset is characterized by one or more of the following thoughts and beliefs:

- "Selecting an internship site is one of the most important decisions I'll ever make in my life."
- "My internship will either open up endless possibilities for my career or stifle my career forever."

The "I acknowledge reciprocity" mindset. This approach is characterized by the following thought and belief:

- "Internship will present me with opportunities to enhance and refine my skills, and I have some talents and ideas that will benefit the site."

How does your current mindset compare to the beliefs presented here? If you most closely identify with the first three mindsets, you probably need an intervention . . . and fast! If your thoughts most closely match the reciprocity mindset, you are on the right track (even if you struggle with some of the others some of the time), and you are likely to become more actualized as you learn more about the process. Clearly, the most grounded and useful stance to take is one that recognizes the interdependence between the intern and the trainers. The promotion of mutuality creates an atmosphere of respect, curiosity, and shared inquiry. It is important for you to realize that, not only are you academically prepared to contribute in meaningful ways and expand your knowledge, you bring your unique life experiences, personality, and perspectives to the training. This is highly valued by sites and supervisors. In addition, you will also have some wonderful opportunities to be exposed to new people, along with new ways of thinking and doing things that will enhance your skills as an emerging practitioner if you choose to take advantage of them. In the end, regardless of how you classify your thoughts, the information that follows in this book will help you become better prepared, more poised, and well positioned, and you will be able to present yourself as you intend.

THE NEXT STEP   Now that you have a grasp on the overarching tasks that you will need to accomplish in the internship application process, it is time to turn your attention to the actual APPIC Application for Internship (AAPI). Chapter 2 presents the elements of the application and provides some suggestions and overarching principles for completing the application.

2 COMPLETING THE APPIC APPLICATION FOR PSYCHOLOGY INTERNSHIPS

Carol Williams-Nickelson

After glancing over the Association of Psychology Postdoctoral and Internship Centers (APPIC) Application for Psychology Internships (the AAPI), you may find the task of completing the application daunting. Keeping track of all your clinical tasks, such as counting and recording each hour of therapy, supervision, group work, charting, assessment, test interpretation, and consulting with peers, just to name a few items, while making note of the age, ethnicity, and diversity status of your clients, can be overwhelming. But it need not be if you break the tasks of gathering information and completing the APPIC into manageable pieces.

This chapter can help you do exactly that. It offers practical guidance and suggestions for completing the application and walks you through a simple example of how to translate clinical hours to the AAPI. This chapter helps you take a detailed inventory of your clinical skills and experiences, but bear in mind that there is *no single correct recipe* for calculating and recording your hours. Several overarching principles are offered to guide you through completing the AAPI in a way that fairly and accurately represents your training history. The chapter includes a few samples of tables and worksheets that can be modified to suit your needs for organizing and tallying your own clinical hours and related experiences. (Many programs provide students with similar worksheets at the beginning of practicum. Under the "Training Resources" section of the APPIC Web site there are additional practicum hours tracking spreadsheets that you may find useful.)

WHAT IS THE AAPI? Not long ago, internship applicants were required to complete a separate application for each internship site they were applying to. There was extreme variability in the style of the applications, the format for recording hours, and in the manner in which essay questions were posed. However, all sites were seeking nearly the same information. To reduce applicant stress, the time required to complete several unique applications, and to create some standardization in the application across APPIC-member internship programs, the AAPI was created. The AAPI consists of two parts: (a) the standardized application form, which is completed by the applicant, and (b) the Academic Program's Verification of Internship Eligibility and Readiness form, which is completed by both the applicant and his or her academic training director.

The AAPI may be downloaded from the APPIC Web site and completed on your computer. Once completed, you will submit the AAPI directly to the internship programs that you wish to apply to, along with any other application materials requested by those programs. Although almost all of the APPIC-member internship programs use the AAPI, a few do not. Therefore, you should check the *APPIC Directory Online* or with each internship program directly for details on specific application procedures and deadlines. As discussed in chapter 1, the online directory and the AAPI are available on the APPIC Web site (www.appic.org).

The AAPI is updated and revised almost every year. *It is very important to download and complete the AAPI for the year in which you are applying for internship.* Generally, there are no *significant* changes in the AAPI each year, but as it is refined to better meet the needs of applicants and internship programs, questions may be modified, instructions may be made more precise, or methods for documenting clinical experiences may change. Be sure to check the APPIC Web site and download the current year's AAPI. Appendix B at the end of this book is a blank 2003–2004 AAPI for your review.[1]

Keep in mind that completing the AAPI is just one part of the process of applying for internship. Although the AAPI is very important, it is only part of a series of items and information that will be used to evaluate your potential and match for a particular site. Referring to the major tasks you will need to accomplish in the internship application process outlined on page 5, you will notice that completing the AAPI is the 8th in a series of 14 steps, or milestones. Keeping the internship tasks in perspective throughout the application process can help you maintain a grounded mindset.

The items that you need to include as part of your completed application are

1. a cover letter
2. the AAPI
3. your curriculum vitae (CV)
4. supplemental materials (transcripts and, on occasion, site-specific items such as additional essay questions or work samples)
5. recommendation letters.

This chapter specifically addresses the AAPI; chapter 4 discusses cover letters, CVs, supplemental materials, and recommendation letters.

COMPLETING THE AAPI

Before you can complete the AAPI, you need to obtain and organize the information that will be reported on the AAPI. Calculating hours and determining the most appropriate categories for recording certain hours is idiosyncratic and ultimately up to you and your clinical training director to negotiate and verify. Students often have a lot of

---

[1]*Note.* The APPIC application as it appears in this book is valid only for the year it is dated. APPIC reserves the right to revise the AAPI at any time and urges users to check the APPIC Web site for the current version. APPIC is not liable for any errors or omissions in the AAPI as it appears in this book.

anxiety around hours issues and look for prescribed information or precise formulas, which is inappropriate and incorrect to include here. As a rule, always consult your director of clinical training if you have any uncertainties about what to record or how to record it.

What follows are general principles and tips—some dos and don'ts—that will help you organize your approach to the AAPI:

- *Do* visit the APPIC Web site (www.appic.org), a comprehensive and excellent resource that will answer most of your general questions and help alleviate concerns and anxiety. A Frequently Asked Questions section is included and you can e-mail Joyce Illfelder-Kaye, PhD, (AAPI Coordinator at jxi1@psu.edu), or the APPIC INTERN-NETWORK listserv with additional questions. Look for updates pertaining to selected searches, internship site changes, stipend comparisons, internship listserv subscription information, and match statistics, along with other important announcements.

- *Don't* send each site the exact same AAPI. Be sure to adjust your 5th essay to fit each site you are applying to. Sites will believe that you are seriously interested if your narrative reflects specific matches to the unique elements of their program. However, it is not required that you adjust the first four essays for each site (see chapter 3 on goals and essays). You can make the match between you and the program explicit in your cover letter and in the fifth essay.

- *Don't* assume that the person reviewing your application knows all about you and your program. Applicants often omit training details that are assumed by the applicant to be universal but actually are unique and important for the internship site to know.

- *Don't* tally all of your hours from logs, calendars, or loose sheets of paper just before sitting down to complete the AAPI. Develop an organized record-keeping system with cumulative totals. You will need to know many details about the setting, age, gender, ethnicity, diversity status, and type of service provided at each practicum site. Start recording these details during your first practicum, or now.

- *Do* organize and review your practica log sheets for accuracy and clarity before completing the AAPI. A mathematical error early on can take hours to find down the road.

- *Don't* count all of your learning experiences as bona fide practica hours. For example, practicing the administration of a test on your partner or a classmate and participating in mock sessions as class demonstrations do not count as practicum hours.

- *Do* be honest in reporting your hours and experiences. (But *don't* become obsessive or paranoid about ensuring that every fraction of an hour is reported accurately and reflected in the proper category!)

- *Do* ask your supervisors and training directors all of your "Can I count . . . ?" hours questions. *They* are responsible for verifying that your practica hours are appropriate and supervised. *You* are responsible for knowing (and reporting) that practica hours are those obtained by (a) practicing your skills; (b) under appropriate supervision; (c) as part of an organized, sequential training experience; (d) with real clients; and (e) in real treatment settings.

- *Do* use your best judgment and realize that you will not be brought up on ethics charges if you make a benign mistake.
- *Don't* inflate your numbers or experiences to match the site.
- *Don't* misrepresent yourself.
- *Do* remember that you are going on internship to learn. This will help reduce feelings of inadequacy as you notice how many blank spaces you are leaving on your application.
- *Do* read the AAPI instructions and follow them. (But *don't* read between the lines, because there is nothing hidden there.) Every attempt has been made to ensure that the instructions are clear, but if you become confused or have an unusual situation, consult with your director of clinical training or e-mail Dr. Illfelder-Kaye or the INTERN-NETWORK listserv to get the answer.
- *Don't* submit your AAPI without having it reviewed and edited by your peers and faculty. *Do* edit your AAPI on more than one occasion and over a period of time.
- *Do* use the "Save" feature frequently as you are completing the AAPI. Some applicants have lost hours of work to power outages or computer lockups.
- *Don't* violate match policies. Simply do not "communicate, solicit, accept, or use any ranking-related information prior to the release of the match results" as outlined in the APPIC rules.
- *Do* ask individuals who will be providing letters of recommendation, "Can you write a letter of strong support?" *Don't* press someone to write a recommendation who articulates any reservations or shows any hesitancy to your request. Unusually vague or bad letters of recommendation can damage your chances of matching to an internship.
- *Do* carefully consider the type of autobiographical information you provide in your essays (AAPI Section 2). Pay attention to your choices about sharing sensitive information such as your ethnic heritage, age, relationship status, socioeconomic status, sexuality, family obligations, visible or invisible disability, and gender. Although highly unlikely, this information may be used in ways you did not intend. Sometimes sharing this information can increase your chances for being highly ranked because the program seeks and respects diversity and they want to know about who you are as a person.
- *Don't* write an autobiographical statement that suggests severe psychopathology. It may not be appropriate to share information about your own hospitalizations or that you selected psychology as a career because you wanted to learn more about your own disorders!
- *Do* remember that this is an evaluative process, and sites are not only using this information to determine your clinical talent and match for reciprocity but also to decide if you are someone who is relatively mentally healthy and someone who they can work with for a year.

CALCULATING AND RECORDING HOURS

The AAPI is divided into two general parts: Part 1 is the standard application form that you complete, and Part 2 is the Program Verification of Internship Eligibility and Readiness form that both you and your director of clinical training complete. Part 1, Section 1 asks for demographic and program information and should be easy to fill in.

Exhibit 2.1. *Sample of Clinical Hours Calculation*

	Client	Number of Sessions	Gender	Age (Adult, Child, Adolescent)	Disability	Ethnicity	Setting (In/Out Patient, CMHC, CC)	Tx Type (Ind., Family, Couple)	Career	Tests
1										
2										
3										
4										
5										
6										
7										
8										
9										
10										
11										
12										
13										
14										
15										
16										
17										
18										
19										
20										
21										
22										
23										
24										
25										

Part 1, Section 2 includes all of your essay questions, which are addressed in chapter 3 in detail. Part 1, Section 3 is also where you record your *doctoral* practicum hours and the point of focus for this discussion.

You will need to separate hours that you accumulated as a doctoral student from those that you earned as part of a terminal master's degree. Hours accumulated while earning a master's degree that was part of a doctoral program should be counted as doctoral practicum hours.

Calculating hours and recording them on the AAPI is one of the most tedious aspects of the application process. There are as many questions about how to count your hours as there are students applying for internship. There is no universally approved or preeminent method for counting and recording your hours on the AAPI. Talk with your director of clinical training to determine if you can include certain hours as program-sanctioned experiences. You may also want to consider establishing regular meetings with classmates who are also applying for internship so that you can complete your applications together and discuss questions and concerns about if and where it is most appropriate to record certain hours.

If you have not done so already, you should immediately begin to develop an organized system for recording your practicum hours as you are accumulating them. This documentation will also be required and useful to you post-internship as you apply for licensure in a particular state. Exhibit 2.1 is an example of an hours table that will probably need to be adapted to match your needs. Whatever system or form you use for recording hours, be sure to also include all of the demographic information called for on the AAPI, including treatment settings; type of service provided; and client age, gender, ethnicity, disability, and diversity status. Some students have clinical work experience outside of their graduate training. Professional work experiences that are separate from practica or program sanctioned work experience may be recorded in section 3, question 8.

You are not expected to have experience in all, or even most, of the areas listed on the AAPI. A comprehensive list of possible clinical activities is provided so that applicants may easily fill in the blanks by transferring their information to the standardized form. Be sure to keep this in mind as you complete the application and notice that there are several categories that you leave blank. Blanks do not infer a deficiency in your training or areas that you should immediately seek experience in; rather, they indicate that the particular training may not be relevant to you or the site, or it may show that you are trainable in certain areas, which sites find appealing.

There are three main categories in which you record your hours.

1. *Intervention and assessment* include
   - individual, group, family and couples therapy, and career counseling
   - school counseling
   - other interventions, such as performance enhancement intake or other structured interviews
   - psychodiagnostic test administration
   - neuropsychological assessment
   - "other psychological experience with students or organizations," such as supervision of other students, outreach, program evaluation, and organizational consultation.
2. *Support activities* include activities spent outside of your therapy hours while still focused on the client, such as
   - chart review
   - writing notes
   - consulting with others about cases
   - video/audio review
   - planning interventions
   - assessment interpretation and report writing
   - didactic training (e.g., seminars, grand rounds).
3. *Supervision* includes one-on-one, group, and peer oversight focused on specific cases.

These three categories are mutually exclusive; that is, a practicum hour may not be counted more than once across any of these main activity categories. When you have an hour that falls under more than one category, select the one category that you feel best captures the experience. If you cannot decide, ask your director of clinical training where to record the hour.

For these three categories, you need to record your experience through November 1. The fourth category allows you to estimate the number of hours you will accumulate before beginning your internship.

Be sure to follow the AAPI instructions for determining what constitutes an hour and how to record hours. In short, hours must

- have been a part of formal academic training and credit
- have been program-sanctioned training experiences,
- have been supervised,
- be listed separately for those acquired as part of your master's degree training and those acquired as part of your doctoral training,
- be calculated by actual hours (although a 50 minute session = 1 practicum hour), and
- be counted only once (i.e., the same hour cannot be recorded or counted in different categories, with the exception of recording diversity).

The AAPI also asks for the number of different individuals, groups, families, and couples that you have provided services to. For example, if you ran a group with 12 individuals in it for 10 weeks, you would record the number 1 in the "# of different groups" category. Finally, you need to record numbers to reflect the diverse demographic population you served. In this category (6e of your AAPI), you may count one person in more than one category.

A basic example is provided here to illustrate how you translate your intervention and assessment experience to the AAPI. If you provided the following services, Exhibit 2.2 illustrates how you would record this information on your AAPI:

- One group for adolescents addressing violence for 12 weeks, 1½ hour per group meeting, with 8 group members
- One group for school-age children addressing social skills for 8 weeks, 1 hour per group meeting, with 10 group members
- Six sessions of couples therapy with the Smiths, 1 hour each session, with 2 people
- Four sessions of couples therapy with the Johnsons, 1 hour each session, with 2 people
- Five family therapy sessions with the Bakers, 1½ hour each session, with 4 family members
- Two career counseling sessions with 1 adolescent, 1½ hour each session
- Eight individual therapy sessions with 8 different adults, 1 hour each session
- Four athletic performance enhancement workshops, 1 hour each session, with 5 people in each workshop
- One family consultation with patient and spouse to discuss medication compliance, 1½ hours.

Section 4 of the AAPI provides you with the opportunity to list your experience with several testing instruments. The list of tests on the AAPI is not exhaustive, and it may be helpful to use a more comprehensive listing of tests to record your testing experiences. Exhibits 2.3 and 2.4 at the end of this chapter provide examples of forms that you may wish to use to document your testing experience with adults and with children and adolescents.

Exhibit 2.2. *Example of Recording Therapy Experience Hours on the AAPI*

	Total No. of Hours Face to Face	No. of Different Individuals, Groups, Couples
a. Individual Therapy		
1) Older Adults		
2) Adults	8	8
3) Adolescents		
4) School-Age		
5) Pre-School Age		
6) Infants/Toddlers		
b. Career Counseling		
1) Adults		
2) Adolescents	3	1
c. Group Therapy		
1) Adults		
2) Adolescents	18	1 (violence group)
3) Children	8	1 (social skills group)
d. Family Therapy	7.5	1 (Baker)
e. Couples Therapy	6	1 (Smith)
	+4	+1 (Johnson)
	10	2
f. School Counseling Interventions		
1) Consultation		
2) Direct Intervention		
3) Other (Specify:)		
g. Other Psychological Interventions		
1) Sports Psychology/Performance Enhancement	4	1
2) Medical/Health-Related Interventions	1.5	1
3) Intake Interview/Structured Interview		
4) Substance Abuse Interventions		
5) Other Interventions (e.g., Milieu therapy, treatment planning with patient present)		

Please describe the nature of the experience(s) listed in g-5:

Assessment is divided into two categories: Adult and Child/Adolescent Testing. Indicate the number of each type of test that you administered and scored in these and any other test categories. You are also asked to record the number of reports written for each type of test administered. "Integrated Report Writing" refers to composing a full psychological assessment (incorporating the results of several tests). Integrated reports must also be divided into the Adult and Child/Adolescent categories. They always include a history and clinical interview and various combinations of at least two of the following:

- objective personality tests
- projective personality tests
- intellectual/cognitive or neuropsychological screening tests
- intellectual, cognitive, or neuropsychological assessments.

PROFESSIONAL CONDUCT AND CERTIFICATION

Sections 5 and 6 are contractual in nature. Sites want to know if there have ever been any complaints, disciplinary action, significant remediation, or unlawful behaviors in your past. Noteworthy is a question asking whether you have ever reneged on a previous APPIC internship match agreement because the APPIC match is a binding agreement. If you answer affirmatively to any of these conduct questions, you must attach an explanation. Finally, provide an original signature for the certification on each application you submit.

SUMMARY

The first step in completing the AAPI is to download the most current form from the APPIC Web site, as the AAPI may change slightly from year to year. It is also wise to note any changes from one year's AAPI to the next so that you are sure to complete the application correctly.

Calculating your clinical hours and experiences is not usually a fun process; it can be frustrating and confusing even for the most organized individual. However, this task must be accomplished to complete the AAPI and to show your sites that you have accumulated valuable experiences that make you a good match. It is important to start the process of organizing and recording your hours as soon as you begin your practicum. Good documentation will help you easily and swiftly transfer your hours to the AAPI. If you have questions about the types of hours that you may count or where to include certain hours on your AAPI, you should always consult with your director of clinical training. Remember, there are no absolute answers regarding how you count and record your clinical experiences. Because of this, working closely with your director of clinical training and simply using your best judgment is critical. After recording your hours, you are ready to begin thinking about your internship and career goals and how to clearly articulate them in your essays. In the next chapter we walk you through the process of goal identification and writing essays that reflect who you are and where you want to be for internship and later in your career.

Exhibit 2.3. *Examples of Assessment Instruments Worksheets: Adult Assessment*

16 PF	Number of Reports Written	Number Administered and Scored
Aphasia Screening Exam		
Basic Personality Inventory		
BASIS		
Beck-Depression Inventory		
Bender Gestalt		
Benton Facial Recognition		
Benton Judgment of Line Orientation		
Benton Visual Retention Test		
Boston Diagnostic Aphasia Examination (BDAE)		
CAI		
Campbell Interest and Skill Survey		
Category Test (Short or Halstead)		
Controlled Oral Word Association Test		
CPI-R		
Draw-A-Person/H-T-P		
Edwards Personal Preference		
GATB		
Gorham's Proverbs		
Halstead-Reitan, Neuropsychology Battery (# Brief, # Full)		
Jackson Personality Inventory		
Luria Nebraska Neuropsychology Battery		
Mattis Dementia Rating Scale		
MicroCog (Computer Battery)		
Millon Behavioral Health Inventory		
Millon Clinical Multi-Axial inventory (Any version)		
MMPI-2 (MMPI)		
Myers-Briggs Type Indicator		
NEO-PI-R		
Norris Educational Achievement Test (NEAT)		
Personality Assessment inventory (PAI)		
POI		
PRF (Personality Research Form-E)		
Rey Osterrieth Complex Figure		
Rorschach (indicate scoring system used)		
Rotter Incomplete Sentences Blank		
Self-Directed Search (SDS)		
Shipley-Institute of Living Scale		
Strong Interest Inventory		
TAT		
Trail-Making Test		
Vocational Card Sorts (e.g., Missouri, etc.)		
WAIS-R		
Wechsler Memory Scale (Revised)		
Wide Range Achievement Test III		
Wisconsin Card Sorting Test		
Word Association Test		
Other:		

How many carefully supervised integrated psychological reports have you written? These would include 1) history, 2) interview, 3) objective personality tests, 4) projective personality tests, and 5) intellectual/cognitive/neuro screening tests:

Total Number of Adult Integrated Reports: _____

Exhibit 2.4. *Example of Assessment Instruments Worksheet: Child/Adolescent Assessment*

	Number of Reports Written	Number Administered and Scored
Adaptive Behavior Scales		
Batelle Developmental Inventory		
Bayley Infant Neurodevelopmental Screener (BINS)		
Bayley Scales of Infant Development - Second Edition (BSID-II)		
Behavioral Assessment Scale for Children (BASC)		
Benton Tests of Neuropsychological Abilities		
California Verbal Learning Test (CVLT)		
CAT		
Childhood Autism Rating Scale - Revised		
Children's Behavior Checklist (CBCL)		
Children's Category Test (CCT)		
Children's Depression Inventory		
Children's Problem Checklist		
Clinical Evaluation of Language Functions (CELF)		
Cognitive Functions Checklist		
Connors Scales (ADD Assessment)		
Continuous Performance Tests (Indicate scoring system used)		
Curriculum-Based Mathematics Assessment		
Curriculum-Based Reading Assessment		
Curriculum-Based Writing Assessment		
Denver Developmental Inventory		
Developmental Test of Visual-Motor Integration		
Diagnostic Interview for Children and Adolescents (DICA)		
Diagnostic Interview Schedule for Children (DISC)		
Differential Ability Scales (DAS)		
Direct Observation Scale		
Expressive One Word Picture Vocabulary Test - Revised		
Finger Tapping Test		
Goodman Lock Box		
Grip Strength Test		
Halstead-Reitan		
Kaufman Assessment Battery for Children (K-ABC)		
Kaufman Brief intelligence Test (K-BIT)		
Kaufman Test of Educational Achievement (K-TEA)		
Kinetic Family Drawing		
Luria Nebraska Children's Revision		
Learning Disabilities Evaluation Scale		
Leiter International Performance Scale - Revised		
Matching Familiar Figures		
McCarthy Scales		
Millon Adolescent Personality inventory		
Minnesota Child Development Inventory		
MMPI-A		
Parenting Stress Index		
Peabody Picture Vocabulary Test - Revised		
Personality Inventory for Children - Revised		
Purdue Pegboard		
Raven's Matrices		
Reitan-Indiana		
Revised Children's Manifest Anxiety Scales (RCMAS)		
Rey Auditory Verbal Learning		

continued next page

Exhibit 2.4. *Continued*

	Number of Reports Written	Number Administered and Scored
Reynolds Adolescent Depression Scale (RADS)		
Roberts Apperception Test for Children		
Rorschach (indicate scoring system used)		
School Consultation		
School Observation		
SCL-90		
Seashore Rhythm Test		
Sentence Instruments		
Social Skills Rating System		
Speech-Sounds Perception Test		
Stanford Binet Intelligence Scale IV		
Stroop Color-Word Test		
Structured Behavioral Assessment		
Symbol Digit Modalities Test		
Symbolic Play Test		
Tell Me A Story (TEMAS)		
Vineland Adaptive Behavior Scales		
Visual Motor Integration Test		
WAIS-R		
Wechsler Individual Achievement Test (WIAT)		
Wide Range Assessment of Memory and Learning		
WISC-III		
WISC-R		
Woodcock Johnson Revised Cognitive Scales (WJ-R Cognitive)		
Woodcock Reading Mastery Tests-Revised (WRMT-R)		
Woodcock-Johnson Revised Tests of Achievement (WJ-R Achievement)		
WPPSI-R		
Other		

How many carefully supervised integrated psychological reports have you written? These would include 1) history, 2) interview, 3) objective personality tests, 4) projective personality tests, and 5) intellectual/cognitive/neuro screening tests:

Total Number of Child/Adolescent Integrated Reports: _____

3 GOALS AND ESSAYS

Shane J. Lopez and Mitchell J. Prinstein

Writing your AAPI essays in a manner that provides a genuine reflection of your aspirations *and* that casts you as a unique budding psychologist is your challenge. How can you be genuine and unique in 500 words or fewer? Well, actually, you have 2,500 words to accomplish this task. Although you should probably explicitly list your professional goals in one of the five essays, you can address these goals indirectly throughout them all. For example, if you were applying to medical centers and you had the goal of "enhancing my scientist–practitioner perspective by practicing in an evidence-based manner and conducting single-case and large sample research when possible," you could discuss your development as a scientist–practitioner in one essay, the process by which you developed your scientist–practitioner orientation as a clinical approach in another essay, identify your attempts to use relevant research when working with diverse client populations in another, describe clinically relevant research goals in the next and, of course, restate the aforementioned goal in your last essay. In this manner, you present your goals in a way that turns them into the active ingredients that are distributed across the essays.

Now, let us take a step back. What *are* your goals? Given that you have almost completed a terminal degree in psychology, we are certain that you are a goal-directed person who knows how to identify your personal quests. So what do you do when you are trying to conjure up your future optimal self? Consider this: When you have listed all of your professional goals, short-term and long-term, divide those into internship goals, early career goals, and mid-career goals. In your essay, do not hesitate to provide the reader with some information about your early career goals so that he or she can see how your internship goals relate to your professional potential. It may be helpful to use the worksheet in Exhibit 3.1 to organize your thoughts about your goals. Once you have refined your internship goals, ask yourself the next two questions as they relate to all of your goals:

1. What are the pathways and opportunities that will serve as the routes to my goal attainment?
2. What are my personal characteristics that will facilitate my goal attainment?

Exhibit 3.1. *Goals Worksheet*

It is important for you to be able to clearly articulate your short- and long-term training and career goals. To do this, you should begin to take inventory now. It is always good to write your ideas down on paper so that you can revisit and revise them regularly.

1. I have a lot of experience in:

2. I am lacking experience in:

3. My supervisors suggest that I should learn more about:

4. Do I want a generalist or specialty experience on internship? Why?

My goals for internship are:

1.

2.

3.

My short-term career goals are:

1.

2.

3.

My longer-term career goals are:

1.

2.

3.

The answers to these two questions will provide information that will enrich your essays and add a personal touch that is often lacking in many AAPI submissions.

It is hoped that you now see how your goals serve as the active ingredients of your AAPI essays. They help tell your story, present your genuine interests and unique qualities, and tie your essays together. The following essay tips should help you create 2,500 words of intrigue. Essay examples are provided at the end of this chapter.

Once you have your goals, the essays are a bit easier to write. You should emphasize your goals and "the match" in each essay, with your response to the fifth question offering a summary and reiteration of the points that you made in essays 1–4. Remember that the admission committee will read hundreds of essays in one sitting. To help them realize that you are a strong match, it is advisable to be very explicit and direct (e.g., "My interest in X matches your rotation in X"). Suggestions for each of the five essays follow.

AUTOBIOGRAPHICAL STATEMENT, ESSAY 1 Essay 1 is often considered the most difficult essay because it also has the most ambiguous purpose. Some sites prefer to get to know you as a person, including both interests in and outside of psychology. The committee may wish to obtain some insight regarding your personality and background and perhaps catch a glimpse of the kind of person you would be during a social interaction. Other sites might be most interested in a professional autobiography, including a discussion of the factors that led to your decision to pursue a career in psychology, a brief review of your experiences, culminating in a discussion of your goals for internship training.

How do you know what the site wants to hear? Unfortunately, you will not know. Some anecdotal evidence suggests that many counseling centers or sites with psychodynamic training may prefer the personal approach while research-oriented or sites with a cognitive–behavioral orientation might prefer a focus on your professional history. Ultimately, this is a decision that you will need to make based on your own comfort level and disposition. Remember, you are not merely looking for a slot; you are looking for a match. If the autobiographical statement truly reflects your style, you are increasing the chances that you will find a true match.

Still, this is a hard task. Exhibit 3.2 provides a list of probes that will help you get started with the autobiographical statement. Additionally, the tips that follow offer more detail.

- *Tell a story*. In other words, describe yourself and your experience in a manner that has a beginning, a middle, and an end. You may wish to start with a depiction of the person you were before graduate school and end with the person you want to be after internship.
- *State your goals*. Explain to the reader where these goals came from. Demonstrate to the committee that these are well-thought-out goals that were developed through a careful review of your past experiences and career objectives. You may even wish to discuss these goals with a supervisor for assistance.
- *Do not restate your curriculum vitae (CV)*. Rather, "walk the reader through" the CV. What are the most important experiences on your CV? What are the themes that have emerged across all of your experiences? Is there something you are especially proud of that you would like to highlight?
- *Talk about the future*. Internship sites know what they are good at and where their interns have gone following training. It will help the committee to know whether they can provide you with the experiences you need if you give them a sense of where you may want to go. Although you may not need to have a clear idea of your future plans (most do not at this stage), you can probably rule in or out at least 2–3 options.

Exhibit 3.2. *Components of a Good Autobiographical Statement*

The following questions will help you construct a cohesive and meaningful autobiographical statement.

1. Who am I? How would others describe me?

2. How did I become interested in psychology?

3. What are my career goals?

4. What experience do I have?

5. What experience am I lacking?

6. How has my experience, or lack thereof, led to the development of my goals for internship? (*Note.* This information should not be a restatement of your vitae. It should be a broad summary of skills you have or have not obtained at this point in your training.)

7. What are the themes (e.g., lots of assessment experience, all child or health oriented, mostly outpatient work) of my training that help to define my educational experiences so far?

8. What is my research experience, and how does this relate to my clinical experience (if applicable)?

9. How might my goals be well matched to the internship site? (Spell this out clearly: "My goal X would be satisfied by your Rotation A.")

Recall that Essay 1, if structured properly, could serve as an organizing theme for the entire set of essays. Hence, you should embed statements about your approach to cases, your experience with diversity, your research goals, and your fit with the site. By constructing the first essay in this manner, your set of essays is more likely to read like a detailed description of you as a professional rather than as a series of fragmented details.

CASE CONCEPTUALIZATION, ESSAY 2

Fear not; this is not a test! It is a chance to articulate the match between you and the training site. Use some of these questions to help you write this essay.

- How do you approach cases theoretically? Be clear about your theoretical orientation to your clinical work.
- What is your approach to assessment? Do you consider differential diagnoses? Do you explore themes in the pattern of your client's relationships or the style in which these experiences are discussed by the client?
- How do you proceed with treatment? Do you measure relevant outcomes as you progress? Do you establish treatment goals? How do you know when treatment is over?
- What are your strengths and weaknesses in case conceptualization? Yes, it is OK to discuss weaknesses (i.e., areas for which you would like to receive additional training). Internship is a training experience, and you should explain how you would like to be trained.

Most important, this essay is used to help you explain the type of training models you were exposed to in your graduate program and the type of training you would like to receive on internship. You may wish to review past experiences by using a case example, or not. You should most certainly discuss future training in an explicit way. If you have chosen a particular site because of their theoretical orientation, then say so! It is hoped that you will be able to integrate some statements regarding your goals and discuss the manner in which your case conceptualization skills will both match the site and be further cultivated by the training experiences that the site has to offer.

DIVERSITY EXPERIENCES, ESSAY 3

Some students have many prior experiences with clients from diverse backgrounds, and some do not. Either way, you can use this statement to discuss your thoughts about diversity and how you think you could, should, or would incorporate these ideas into clinical practice and research. Address the following questions when planning your essay.

- What does diversity mean to you?
- Describe a situation in which you recognized that diversity was important to consider. Remember, diversity can refer to demographic, geographic, or ideological heterogeneity among your past clients.
- Have your experiences led you to develop specific (primary or supplemental) training goals related to diversity?
- How do these goals match the opportunities offered at this training site?
- What are your multicultural counseling competencies? What are your weaknesses in this area?

RESEARCH EXPERIENCE, ESSAY 4

This essay may not be applicable to all. If you are applying to a research-oriented program, then you will want to discuss your past research experiences; the themes of your research program; your dissertation, including its (current and expected) completion status; and your interests regarding research training before and after internship. You also may want to describe the programmatic nature of your research.

If you are not pursuing a career in research, you may still have experiences that you wish to convey. You also may wish to discuss how these research experiences have informed your clinical work. Provide a specific example or perhaps discuss a theory with clinical application.

If this is the first essay in which you are discussing your training goals and how you perceive that these goals match the opportunities offered at the training site, then you need to go back and revise essays 1–4! Let this essay serve as a brief reiteration of your training goals and a more specific articulation of the exact rotations, didactic seminars, philosophies, supervisors, and other site qualities that directly match your interests. Here are some suggestions.

- *Use strong language.* If you think that this site is a unique or exceptional match, then say so. Convince the reader that training at his or her site would be ideal to help you achieve your specific training goals.
- *List names.* Yes, this will mean that you will need to rewrite this statement, in part or whole, for each application. However, if the other essays generally state your goals for training overall, then Essay 5 may be the only one that you need to substantially revise for each site. It is a good idea to list the rotations and supervisors that are of greatest interest. You do not have to commit to anything but instead make clear that several exciting opportunities match your interests, and you easily could be happy with a combination of the experiences offered at the site.
- *Be authentic.* Do not state a match if there is not one. Remember, you are not just looking for a slot, not just a match but the *best* match. If you say you are interested in something that you are not or if you exaggerate the level of your interest, you are not only doing a disservice to the site and the other applicants but most certainly to yourself.
- *Be enthusiastic!* You have been in the same graduate program for at least 4 years. This is a chance to go out into the world and establish a professional identity beyond the walls of your school. This is the beginning of everything that led you to pursue graduate training so many years ago. Sure, you may be tired now, distressed about your dissertation, worried about obtaining an internship match. Yes, you may have questioned your career choice several times over the past 4+ rigorous years of training. But now you are almost there, and your career is about to change forever. Remember how excited you were when you were admitted to graduate school and thought about a career as a practitioner, researcher, consultant, or teacher? Reclaim that enthusiasm, if only for a moment! And then write this essay.

SUMMARY

Many applicants view the AAPI essays as a major roadblock to completing applications for internship. Indeed, the task of writing five stories about your personal and professional selves can be intimidating. By clarifying your professional goals prior to starting the essays you can connect the short stories into one longer, more powerful story, and you can increase the likelihood of communicating your fit with programs. Now that you have written a stellar and compelling set of essays, it is time to think about your supplementary materials and your approach to the interview process; these are discussed in the next two chapters.

Sample Essay Responses to the 2003–2004 AAPI

Please note: All biographical and other identifying information has been removed from these essays. Remember, these examples are not necessarily ideal or flawless, but they provide a good sample of the types of essays former applicants have submitted.

Sample Responses to Question 1

1. Please provide an autobiographical statement. (There is no "correct" format for this question. Answer this question as if someone had asked you, "Tell me something about yourself." It is an opportunity for you to provide the internship site with some information about yourself. It is entirely up to you to decide what information you wish to provide along with the format in which to present it.)

Applicant A

As I ponder my life thus far, a quotation by William Hazlit (1778) comes to mind, "A strong passion . . . will insure success, for the desire of the end will point out the means." Ambition, passion, service, motivation, and persistence are words that have dominated my life's work and created my life's path. These sustaining qualities have been both influenced and maintained by significant individuals and by experiences throughout the years.

I am the oldest of a family of four children raised in a small poor rural town. Heavily influenced by a Russian Judaic background and Native American spirituality, our family struggled to fit into the social mold. Despite the obstacles that surrounded my childhood years, my parents were supportive and encouraged me to strive to reach my full potential. My family's constant belief that you can create your destiny and their belief in my talents and ability to contribute to the healing profession planted the first seeds of motivation and passion for service.

Growing up in a family of healers, I quickly discovered the value of providing assistance to those in need. Thus, when I was in sixth grade I made the decision to pursue a career as a psychologist. In college, my first experience in the field was working with emotionally disturbed and sexually abused young women. In addition, it was at this time that a close friend was assaulted. I saw clearly for the first time the power of a psychologist's work, and my commitment to women's issues, trauma recovery, and my career path was solidified. In continued pursuit of my passion and ambition for service, I sought a master's degree. It was during my master's program that fervor for research and for the substance use field developed. However, this program also created a thirst for more knowledge and experience. Thus, I enrolled in a doctoral program in counseling psychology.

I have developed my skills, interests, and identity as a mental health professional through a variety of mentoring relationships and educational and training experiences. These relationships and experiences have helped me gather the strength and fortitude to trust myself and to utilize my strengths. They have also helped maintain my commitment, dedication, and passion for psychology. In addition, my relationships and experiences have also taught me the necessity in balancing my career aspirations with a personal life. To rejuvenate, I enjoy time with my animals, hiking, meditating, or reading a favorite philosopher. Additionally, I love to travel, to dance, and to participate in a variety of advocacy groups.

Hence, not only have my passion and commitment to my work been unwavering, it has been the impetus for a variety of meaningful professional and personal experiences. Thus far, I feel proud of where my passion and dedication have brought me and feel excited about where they might take me. I look forward to the prospect of having them bring the opportunity to personally introduce myself to you.

Applicant B

I certainly cannot say that I expected to become a clinical psychologist from an early age. Indeed, growing up in a hard-working family in Town, State, where my father and older brothers are mechanics, a career in psychology was well off my anticipated path. However, I was introduced to clinical psychology as a high school senior and was immediately fascinated by the models I learned about that explained different facets of human behavior. These models greatly facilitated my understanding of the functions, orderliness, and predictability of many behaviors, and the applications appeared endless. More recently, I have learned to use clinical psychology not only as a means to understand the actions of others, but more importantly, as a vehicle for helping to improve people's functioning and mental health, which I think is really the most valuable thing one has.

The significance of accurately evaluating and treating psychopathology became particularly clear to me during a college internship in a locked psychiatric unit for violent inpatients during a semester abroad. This unique experience confirmed my interest in clinical work, but also triggered a whole set of questions in my mind that remain at the center of my clinical and research interests: Why do some people repeatedly engage in aggressive behaviors, while others are compelled to hurt themselves? Why are some virtually paralyzed by anxiety and depression? How can we change the behaviors of those who want help? What about those who do not? After consulting my supervisors and visiting the library, I was intrigued and motivated to learn that the answers to such crucial questions remain, to a large extent, unknown.

Over the next several years, I deliberately sought out a wide range of clinical and research positions in the mental health field that approached the understanding and treatment of these problems from a number of different perspectives. Through each of these unique experiences, I consistently realized the value and importance of using systematic observation and evaluation as a means of studying these phenomena and developing effective treatments. Consequently, I chose to attend the doctoral program at X University because of its strong commitment to the scientist–practitioner training model. This training has taught me not only to be a consumer of clinical research, but also to use scientific methods to continually evaluate the treatments I provide, and to actively contribute to the larger scientific and clinical community. For instance, I have completed several clinically relevant studies on the development and treatment of aggression, anxiety, and suicidal behaviors. Moreover, my NIMH-funded dissertation research is focused on evaluating the effectiveness of a therapy preparation component, which I developed based on recent research conducted at our clinic, to increase participation and therapeutic change in child therapy. Such an interaction between science and practice is what continues to excite me about this work and is a consistent theme in my approach to clinical and research activities.

I look forward to internship as a valuable opportunity to continue to obtain the best training experience possible in order to strengthen the foundation on which I will build my career as a clinician, researcher, and teacher. I am strongly interested in the internship program at Your-Site because it offers the most logical continuation of my scientist–practitioner training, as well as exciting opportunities to expand on my knowledge of evidenced-based treatments and to continue to apply these interventions to a wide variety of clients (e.g., children, adolescents, and adults) in diverse settings (e.g., outpatient and inpatient). I hope I will have the opportunity to receive this training at Your-Site and to be as much of a benefit to the internship program as I know it will be to me.

Applicant C

My interest in clinical psychology began with a summer class in introductory psychology. I found the course material captivating and wanted to learn as much as I could about the field of psychology, both experientially as well as in the classroom. As an undergraduate, I volunteered to work at a shelter for abused children. The following year I volunteered in a sheltered workshop at the State Industries for the Blind assisting individuals with visual impairments to learn to live independently as well as gain work experience.

Following graduation, I pursued a master's degree in Guidance and Counseling. I had the opportunity to use my educational training to gain a breadth of work experiences that ranged from working in a private psychiatric hospital, to working as a case worker with individuals from diverse cultural and socioeconomic backgrounds and, later, planning a variety of human services for diverse populations throughout State X. My career path has led me through some unique experiences including working in more political environments such as the Office of the Governor, Chief of Staff for the Director of the State X Department of Economic Security, and Chief of Staff for the Executive Director of the State X Board of Regents. These positions provided me the opportunity to use and further develop exceptional analytical, problem-solving, negotiation, and facilitation skills. I found my work in the political arena to be fascinating and extremely valuable—it certainly challenged my thinking about human behavior. As a result, I have a better understanding of political relationships and strategies, policy development and analysis, as well as the State's legislative and budget processes.

I have been married for 26 years. Family has been a priority for me; my husband and I have raised two sons. During this time, I also set educational and other life goals. Since my children have matured and my husband has completed his PhD, I found myself in a position to be able to return to school to complete my doctoral degree. I found my studies in psychology to be much more meaningful because of my varied life experiences. Like most people, I have encountered challenging situations. I have found the inner strength to face these challenges. While I am grateful for the many successes in my life, I have learned to appreciate the benefits of insight and growth gained from difficulty and adversity. These experiences have been especially helpful in providing the insight and abilities necessary to assist others in facilitating the changes they want or need to make in their lives.

I have had a rich path of experiences that have brought me full-circle to my original goal of returning to school to complete a doctoral degree in clinical psychology. I look forward to beginning my internship year and working with supervisors to further develop my clinical skills.

Applicant D

I have been interested in a career as a clinical psychologist for many years because of the opportunities it affords for both intellectual and emotional stimulation. Since early high school, I have worked with children and adults with various emotional, physical, and cognitive challenges. Initially, I was drawn to the field because of my interest in working with and learning from people and my fascination with human development and change. Consequently, I began to volunteer and work at hospitals and distress centers in XXXX and XXXX. I worked with children and adolescents with physical and developmental disabilities as well as severe emotional and cognitive impairments and undergraduate students in crisis. These experiences taught me the value of psychological interventions and the tenacity of the human spirit and confirmed my interest in being a practitioner. In addition, these experiences showed me how little I knew about the reasons people develop emotional problems and the mechanisms for change. It was my desire to learn more about the continuum of human functioning, and cognition in particular, which encouraged my interest in research. The blend of these interests made the scientist–practitioner model ideal for me, so I began to volunteer and work in psychology labs gaining research and practical experience in anxiety and eating disorders (practica and research areas that I continue to explore in graduate school).

As I have gained experience in the field, I find myself increasingly drawn to research and the process of questioning the world around us. I am interested in the ways we can more effectively adapt to our surroundings and alter our thinking processes to improve our functioning. I have particularly enjoyed the interplay between therapy and research. Along these lines, I am excited to be coauthor on a book that is currently in preparation and will be published by XXX Publications on treatment planning. Our goal is to advise students and practitioners on how to make evidence-based treatment planning, goal setting, and assessment feasible. We attempt to impart the value of using an empirical perspective to evaluate individual clients' progress in treatment.

In addition, I really enjoy teaching and mentoring. Specifically, I love exchanging ideas with students and sharing excitement about the research and practice of clinical psychology. Over the past year, I have been the Assistant Director of the University Psychological Services Clinic, which has allowed me to help train our incoming clinical graduate students and supervise them conducting intake evaluations.

I have been very fortunate in the scientist–practitioner training I have received at X University. The program has motivated me to develop my skills for an academic career as a researcher, clinician, teacher, and supervisor. At this time, I look forward to the opportunity during internship to (a) work with more severely ill and diverse populations than I have previously, (b) to expand my skills in cognitive–behavioral techniques and the application of therapeutic approaches that are new to me, and (c) the chance to collaborate on new research projects.

Sample Responses to Question 2

(Note: This question is phrased differently in the current AAPI, but the information being sought is the same.)

2. Describe how your approach to case conceptualization and assessment informs your interventions. Pay particular attention to articulating your theoretical orientation, strategies for evaluation, and the specific interventions that you would use.

Applicant A

Innate empathy, genuine concern, and compassion are personal attributes that I bring to my role as a trainee. These characteristics have been the foundation on which my clinical strengths have emerged and continue to develop. I am able to aptly identify client strengths and resiliencies that can be used as anchoring points for productive client change, leaving clients with a sense of empowerment and dignity in situations that may appear hopeless, stressful, overwhelming, or defeating. I seek to establish a cooperative environment that allows for the exchange of ideas and expertise in the therapy process. I used diagnosis as a mechanism for client change and insight.

Rather than offering a diagnosis as the answer to the client's problem situation, I prefer to use diagnosis as a springboard for generative therapeutic conversation. This approach is consistent with my theoretical orientation.

Postmodern assumptions that include social constructivism and narrative approaches to therapy inform the way I think about and talk with clients. I organize my thinking through the metaphors of narration (or storytelling) and social construction. I conceptualize problems as being separate from the person experiencing the difficulties. Many problems are stories that clients construct through social interaction. These socially constructed realities provide the beliefs, practices, words, and experiences from which clients create their life stories and constitute themselves. The meanings that clients attribute to the events and experiences in their lives create their reality. Because meaning is created through individuals in conversation, new meaning and a new reality can be introduced by changing the stories clients tell themselves. Every client has his or her own version of truth with its own inherent logic. Clients interpret their experiences based upon their version of truth, and these realities, or truths, can be organized, maintained, or changed through modifying the types of conversations to which clients are engaged in or exposed.

Similarly, assessment can be useful in offering one possible life story for clients to accept, reject, or change. Given the dynamic nature of assessments, these tools can help provide direction for the client and therapist in determining which aspects of the client's story they wish to retain and which they would like to change. From a consultative perspective, helping clients create alternate meanings for symptoms creates opportunities for change and intervention rather than restricting options.

For me, good clinical interviews determine the appropriate diagnostic tests to administer and the subsequent use of those tests in understanding and treating the client's presenting problems. I do not use any predetermined set of tests for every client I see, as the nature of the client's problems and needs will dictate the tests and interventions used.

Applicant B

My approach to case conceptualization, evaluation, and treatment planning is primarily behavioral and cognitive–behavioral in nature and is strongly influenced by the principles of learning (e.g., operant and classical conditioning paradigms). While learning theory is most often associated with behavioral and cognitive–behavioral treatments, the basic elements of this theoretical framework are pervasive in cognitive, psychodynamic, humanistic, and other treatment approaches, strengthening the appeal and the applicability of this approach.

The first, and perhaps most important, step in my application of this approach to a clinical case is the use of comprehensive, reliable, and valid assessments that draw on multiple methods and informants and that continue to test, inform, and guide the case conceptualization and intervention plan throughout treatment. My next step is the collaborative development of a clear and specific list of presenting problems and an evaluation of the clinical severity and impairment associated with each problem. At the center of my case conceptualization is a generation of hypotheses about the function of each problem behavior, including an analysis of factors that may be causing or maintaining these problems (e.g., antecedents and consequences of each behavior) and about the interrelation of the presenting problems.

My treatment plan follows directly from my primary case conceptualization. On the most basic level, whatever maladaptive learning has occurred must be "unlearned" (e.g., an association between a feared object and anxiety is weakened via exposure) and whatever adaptive learning has not occurred must be learned (e.g., prosocial behavior is increased when followed by positive reinforcement). Since assessment and treatment are inseparable elements from my perspective, the continuous evaluation of the target problems is a critical component of my approach. The information provided by frequent and continued assessments is used to test the effectiveness of the intervention and to modify my conceptualization and treatment plan as necessary. In addition, my treatment plan incorporates evidence-based treatment techniques or treatment packages when available and is based directly on the principles of learning whenever possible.

I particularly enjoy working from a learning perspective because this approach is straightforward, flexible, parsimonious, widely applicable, and evidence-based. I look forward to receiving additional training in the use of evidence-based evaluation and treatment procedures during internship. Indeed, I am uniquely interested in the internship program at Site because of the attention given to such approaches in didactic instruction, clinical training, and case supervision, as well as the rich opportunities to interact with clinicians and supervisors working from a wide range of case conceptualization approaches to which I have had less exposure (such as psychodynamic and interpersonal approaches), as these are my main goals for the internship year. Moreover, the application of such approaches to the treatment of impulsive, anxious, and depressed children and adolescents, such as that offered in the Site Center rotations at the Institute for the Study of Psychological Service and the Anxiety and Mood Disorders Service, are a direct match with my previous training and current interests, and I look forward to the chance to learn more about these opportunities.

Applicant C

My therapeutic approach tends to be integrative based on the contextual needs of the client. In addition, I believe the success of therapy is dependent upon establishing an excellent therapeutic relationship between therapist and client. Two factors I consider essential in conceptualizing a case and tailoring the best method of treatment include (a) cultural background and (b) level of development. Culture influences an individual's worldview. It is important for psychologists to understand and respect the views of the individual in order to successfully facilitate treatment. When working with a Latino client who is strongly family oriented, for example, I may explore whether the client would like family members directly involved in the therapeutic process and, if so, rely more heavily on a family systems approach. Understanding the culture of individuals also helps me understand their values, cognitive schema and, ultimately, their behavior. The developmental level of the individual is also an important factor that may indicate contextual issues an individual may bring to therapy. Level of development may also influence the method of treatment. Play therapy, for example, may be a good fit for treatment of young children, while group therapy may be beneficial for adolescents.

My doctoral training has provided exposure to various theoretical models and therapeutic methods including Client-Centered Therapy, Psychoanalytic Therapy, Cognitive–Behavioral Therapy (CBT), Group Psychotherapy, Marital and Family Therapy, and Child Psychotherapy. While CBT is the theoretical model with which I have the most clinical experience, I welcome the opportunity to have additional clinical training in other models.

In terms of case conceptualization using CBT, I generally assume that the individual's core beliefs are ultimately affecting behavior. I find it helpful to use a collaborative approach involving the individual through every step of case conceptualization. After ascertaining the presenting problem, we develop a comprehensive problem list across various domains such as medical/biological, interpersonal, financial, employment, educational, and personal safety. We then explore core beliefs the individual holds that may be causing the identified problems and facilitate discussion to identify situations that may be activating the core beliefs that are problematic. Based on this information, I develop hypotheses that may explain the interrelationship between problems, core beliefs, and resulting behavior. In addition, I gather information about early history including interpersonal relationships between the individual and parents/family or other significant individuals, which may explain how the individual acquired core beliefs. Ultimately, we develop a treatment plan that identifies the desired outcomes of therapy. It is also helpful to identify potential obstacles to treatment in the event the client is resistant or terminates treatment. Intervention strategies would focus primarily on changing core beliefs.

I recognize that many factors influence an individual's behavior. In some cases it may be necessary to gather additional information including interviews with family members or other significant individuals, reviewing available records, or conducting a psychological assessment. These sources may be especially helpful in diagnosis and case conceptualization.

Sample Responses to Question 3

3. Please describe your experience and training in work with diverse populations. Your discussion should display explicitly the manner in which multicultural/diversity issues influence your clinical practice and case conceptualization.

Applicant A

One of the most exciting aspects of living in America is its cultural diversity. Our country is made up of people with unique and exciting cultural histories and experiences. Consequently, I find each session with a client to be an example of multicultural therapy. Otherwise, I would be in danger of ignoring my own upbringing, my values, my training, and my responsibility to my clients. Indeed, I constantly strive to experience my clients', supervisees', and students' perspectives and to understand their personal culture.

Throughout my training, I have gained experience with a variety of clients from different backgrounds. I have worked with numerous African American clients in therapy, diagnostic assessment, and intake sessions. Additionally, I have experience with Native Americans, Asian Americans, Hispanics, Biracial clients, and clients with physical disabilities. Furthermore, living in Kentucky also allowed the opportunity to work with many individuals from Appalachia. I have found my training experiences with these clients enlightening, as I had no experience with this culture prior to moving to Kentucky. My cultural awareness was quickly raised as I was faced with the reality that this cultural group had a completely different worldview and understanding of relationships. Consequently, I clearly realized that diversity and multicultural issues can extend beyond those attached to ethnicity and race.

My own experience with a multicultural background and my training has helped to shape my views on diversity and multicultural therapy. I believe it is important to understand the social location of every client. I conceptualize clients through a social constructive perspective. Thus, I believe that race and culture are in part a socially constructed phenomenon. Societal messages and power structures can help shape an individual's identity and worldview. Therefore, when assessing a client's presenting problems, I gather information about their personal and cultural understanding and identity. As a cognitive–behaviorist, I often look at their belief system and the messages they have received from members of their culture and from society in general. I seek to empower clients, allowing them to challenge the beliefs that they find limiting and affirm the beliefs that they find imperative to their identity. I enjoy exploring and integrating such things as their acculturation process and cultural identity development. I draw upon the literature and my client's experience in creating a collaborative treatment plan that will help the client achieve their therapy goals. Finally, I often ponder the possibility of bringing in indigenous healers or support.

Although I believe I have a sound foundation in issues of diversity and multicultural therapy, I will always continue to strive for more knowledge, awareness, and experiences in this area, as it is close to my heart. It is my aspiration that during my internship training and beyond it that I can continue to learn and grow in this area. It is with hope that as I do gain more knowledge and experience that I can become more knowledgeable of and facile with diverse populations.

Applicant B

I am fortunate to have had a wealth of clinical and training experiences with diverse populations up to this point in my career, and I look forward to building on these experiences during internship. At X University, diversity training is an integral part of the course curriculum and clinical training. For instance, we have a weekly, semester-long seminar series focusing on clinical research relevant to ethnic and cultural diversity presented by eminent researchers from around the country. In addition, issues of socioeconomic, ethnic, and cultural diversity have been explicitly addressed in each of my clinical practica at X University, through which I evaluated and treated a diverse client population from the City, State, area. Also, as an active member of my department's Diversity Committee, I am helping to develop methods of diversifying our own graduate student population and training experience.

The clinical experiences I had before graduate school also provided the opportunity to work with very unique and diverse populations. For instance, in Europe, I worked at a psychiatric hospital serving a large, urban catchment area and had a violent, severely ill, and socio-culturally diverse population. In X City, my experiences ranged from working for a corporate managed health care organization serving professional clientele to working as an intake clinician at X Outpatient Service, a homeless shelter for an "under 21" population who were primarily low-income minority adolescents. These experiences with truly diverse populations have prepared me well for future work in a range of clinical settings.

As a result of my training and clinical experiences, issues of ethnic, cultural, and socioeconomic diversity influence my case conceptualization, assessment, and treatment procedures in several ways. First, I routinely evaluate whether (and how) a client or family's cultural beliefs influence their view of the presenting problems. For example, ethnic and cultural differences in parenting style (e.g., permissiveness vs. strictness) have been well documented and can often influence a parent's perception of their child's behavior problems. Second, I similarly evaluate whether a client or family's cultural beliefs influence their view of psychotherapy in general, or the specific treatment plan in particular. For instance, some of my research has demonstrated that African American and Latino families tend to view psychotherapy as less credible than European American families and that this view may lead to decreased participation in treatment. Third, I evaluate whether a client or family's cultural beliefs influence the method of treatment delivery. For instance, I recently worked with a family from the Dominican Republic in which the success of the intervention was greatly facilitated by actively involving the father in treatment planning and implementation, since he was the head of the household and yielded a strong influence over the rules of the house and the disciplinary practices with the children. I believe that a failure to recognize this cultural dynamic may have led to a lack of treatment adherence or attrition from treatment all together.

I believe it is essential for my development as a clinician and researcher that I continue to receive training and experiences in the treatment of diverse populations. Indeed, this diversity is one of the many things I enjoy about City, State, and is one of the reasons I am enthusiastic about the possibility of participating in the internship program at Site.

Applicant C

Diversity is an expansive term with far-reaching implications. It is a term that is often used to reflect differences in culture and race but may also reflect divergence in gender, spiritual beliefs, age, sexual orientation, and socioeconomic status. My doctoral program at X University is dedicated to integrating issues of diversity in all courses. Each course emphasized the implications of diversity to the specific topic (e.g., how psychopathology manifests in adults from other cultures; how gender differences affect adult and child development). One course I found particularly helpful in understanding the worldviews of various cultures was entitled "Treatment of Diverse Populations." Through this and other courses, I learned I am more successful in my relationships with others—whether clients, acquaintances, or friends—if I take the time to understand their views of the world. This training has challenged my thinking about perspectives that differ from my own and has greatly improved my preparation to become a clinician.

I have had the opportunity to work with diverse populations throughout my practicum and other work experiences. As a case worker for the City of X and as a practicum student working with the X County Head Start program, for example, I worked with children and families of Latino, African American, and Caucasian descent. All individuals and families were of low socioeconomic status and were often faced with various life-challenging situations. I worked primarily with people in their homes, which provided me the unique opportunity to experience them within their own environments. Cultural values and beliefs were often essential factors in the therapeutic process.

I have also worked with people of various ages and abilities. My practicum experience with the X Unified School District focused primarily on psychological assessment of children and adolescents ages 6 to 15 years. Students represented various cultural and socioeconomic backgrounds. They often had learning and other disabilities. At the X County Head Start program, I worked with preschool children and their families. Children were often first- or second-generation U.S. citizens; Spanish was frequently the primary language of their parents. As a Case Worker for the City of X, I worked primarily with adults including a number of elders. Some individuals had physical illnesses or disabilities and were concerned about health care as well as maintaining independence in their own homes. As a psychiatric assistant in an acute care private psychiatric hospital, my work focused on adults and young adults with serious mental health issues. I also ran a sensory stimulation group for elderly people with dementia.

Overall, these experiences have given me a greater understanding of divergent perspectives and a rich exposure to various cultural values, spiritual beliefs, gender role differences, views and needs of different age groups, as well as the day-to-day challenges faced by individuals of low socioeconomic status.

Applicant D

Working with minority populations and clients with unique needs is one of the opportunities I have particularly enjoyed in my graduate training. Consequently, I am eager to add to these experiences during internship. Since being in State, I have done a number of evaluations looking at the prevalence of posttraumatic stress disorder and substance abuse among inner-city children whose ethnic origin was predominantly Hispanic and African American. In addition, University's clinical program has made diversity issues an important part of our training. For example, we have a semester-long speaker series focusing on clinical research relevant to ethnic and cultural diversity, and our adult assessment class includes a series of readings emphasizing cultural sensitivity in assessment and treatment.

Before graduate school I had the chance to work with diverse age groups, including conducting interviews with elderly persons in XXXX and conducting interviews with children with anxiety and mood disorders, as well as adolescents with eating disorders while in XXXX. Additionally, while volunteering at a crisis line, I spoke with many undergraduate students who were struggling with issues of sexuality, including coming out as a gay man or lesbian. Further, while in XXXX, I worked at a respite center for children with a range of physical and developmental disabilities.

I have found that my work with varied populations has challenged me to think more carefully about my own biases and the culturally bound assumptions I make about appropriate treatment outcome expectations and diagnostic formulations. For example, I have been challenged to consider how non-Western cultures think about ideal body shapes and the cultural meanings of food in eating disorders and weight loss management groups. More generally, I am learning that although I may know about a particular diagnosis, it is the individual client who is the real expert on what he or she is experiencing. It is my responsibility to try and understand their perspective and to help them learn ways to function more effectively in their unique environment. I try to work with clients on generating solutions to problems that meet their particular needs and which can feasibly be implemented given their background. In addition, I have been challenged to think about how particular subcultures may experience and report emotional problems differently, such as the tendency for non-Western cultures to emphasize somatic complaints in depression, and to consider using culturally appropriate measures. I find that diversity issues need to be considered at all stages of treatment, from initial diagnosis (because of differences in disorder phenomenology and symptom reporting) to treatment structure and evaluation.

These experiences (and challenges!) have made me eager to further my training with multicultural and diversity issues during internship. This will be important not only for the development of my clinical skills but also critical for writing the book on treatment planning. We are motivated to make it useful for diverse populations and treatment settings. I find the opportunity to learn from people who have different life experiences from my own to be one of the greatest benefits of clinical practice.

Sample Responses to Question 4

(Note: This question is phrased differently in the current AAPI, asking for a description of your research <u>experience</u> and interests. The information sought is essentially the same.)

4. Please describe your research interests.

Applicant A

As someone who embraces the scientist–practitioner model, my clinical interests and research interests are complementary. I have sought clinical training and a degree specialty in dual diagnosis, with trauma and substance use being the main foci. In addition, I have conducted research on, among other things, correlates of substance use and trauma, motivation and substance use, treatment utilization and substance use, and gender and sensation-seeking differences in substance use.

When searching for a topic for my dissertation, I attempted to merge my identities as a researcher and clinician. Consequently, I have a dissertation goal of documenting the differential effects of rape among addicted women on treatment utilization, treatment motivation, perceived barriers to treatment, and problem severity. I believe that there is a lack of research and knowledge of the difference rape makes in treatment for women in the addiction field. The purpose of my dissertation is twofold. First, I intend to show that rape decreases motivation for addiction treatment, causes more perceived barriers to treatment, decreases treatment utilization, and increases different types of problem severity. Second, I intend to explore some qualitative questions regarding their motivation for treatment. The latter section intends to explore more of the interplay of their symptoms and their motivation for various types of treatment. The main motivation construct in this study is based on Prochaska and DiClemente's model. I have chosen to apply for a grant to fund my project and to utilize a publication format for my dissertation write-up, and I intend to have at least two manuscripts suitable for publication as an end result.

I have developed a strong knowledge base in statistical and research methodology as a result of my educational career. I have worked on many research projects performing a myriad of duties ranging from running subjects, to data entry, to questionnaire development, to data analysis. Consequently, I have developed a strong research identity. Additionally, as a scientist–practitioner, I believe that research should inform clinical practice and clinical practice should inform research. Therefore, I am committed to publishing and presenting results of my psychological research at national and local conferences. I am currently working on multiple manuscripts that will be submitted for publication prior to my beginning internship. Additionally, I am committed to publishing the results of my dissertation. I am dedicated to presenting and publishing my work because I believe it will provide valuable information to clinicians and other researchers.

As someone who aspires to future research in trauma, posttraumatic stress, and substance use, as related to treatment engagement, completion, and efficacy, I believe I can further develop my research skills through additional research and clinical mentorship.

Therefore, I continuously seek clinical and research experiences related to these interests to help inform my research and clinical future.

Applicant B

My research focuses broadly on the etiologies; assessment; and treatment of impulsive, aggressive, and self-injurious behaviors in children and adolescents. These behaviors are widespread and often cause serious impairment and physical harm, yet they are not well-studied or understood, particularly in children and adolescents. Given the limited research on these topics to date, much of my research has attempted to answer fundamental questions related to the development and assessment of these conditions. For instance, my master's thesis examined affective, behavioral, and cognitive aspects of child suicide. Other studies I have completed examined more extreme forms of impulsive and aggressive behavior such as parent-directed physical aggression in clinic-referred children and severe acts of violence in Vietnam veterans.

Although these and other studies of mine have explored a range of factors associated with aggressive and self-injurious behaviors, I have become particularly interested in the role of emotion dysregulation in the occurrence of these behaviors. For instance, I found that the primary reason given for self-mutilation by adolescent psychiatric inpatients is that it serves to help regulate their emotional experiences. Also, frustration intolerance, a related construct, was a significant predictor of parent-directed physical aggression in children in another study. The significant role of emotion dysregulation in the occurrence of aggressive and self-injurious behaviors has led to a secondary interest in other conditions characterized by problems with emotion regulation, such as anxiety and depressive disorders. Obviously, there is still much work to be done in addressing fundamental questions related to the assessment and prediction of impulsive, aggressive, and self-injurious behaviors, as well as on emotion dysregulation, and one arm of my research will continue to focus in these areas.

More recently, the scope of my research has expanded to focus on the treatment of impulsive and aggressive behaviors in children and adolescents. I completed a second master's thesis that included a review of recent progress in the treatment of child conduct problems and concluded that there is a significant gap in our understanding of the mechanisms through which these treatments work or what factors moderate their efficacy/effectiveness. My dissertation, for which I received an NIMH National Research Service Award, is addressing one factor that pertains to the latter issue: namely, the role of parents' participation (i.e., attendance and adherence) in their child's treatment. More specifically, I am conducting (1) a descriptive study examining several potential predictors (e.g., parent motivation and expectancies for treatment) and outcomes of parent participation; as well as (2) a randomized, controlled clinical trial testing a brief (one-session) intervention designed to increase parent participation by identifying and removing potential barriers to parent participation at the start of treatment. At a very basic level, the efficacy of our current treatments—particularly those that are skills-based—may be weakened if clients do not attend or adhere to treatment. Accordingly, this line of research may produce a means of improving the therapeutic outcome of a range of clinical conditions and client populations.

Given my interest in continuing these, and related, lines of clinical research, I am extremely excited about the possibility of participating in the Site child and adolescent internship program. Several of the clinical rotations offered, such as those at the Institute for the Study of Psychological Service and the Anxiety and Mood Disorders Service, as well as the opportunity to work in the psychiatric inpatient unit, match closely with my goals for clinical training as well as with my current and future research interests.

Applicant C

I have a wide variety of research interests. I plan to continue to study and update my doctoral research comparing licensure requirements across professions that was published in the Date X edition of *APA Journal X*. Findings of this study indicated that the amount of time to become a licensed psychologist far exceeds most other professions reviewed (e.g., attorneys, general family physicians, dentists, veterinarians). In addition, median incomes for psychologists are substantially lower than many other professions. Specifically, I would like to expand this research by studying the effectiveness of postdoctoral experience for practicing psychologists as well as including additional professions in the study.

I have also begun to study axiological differences across generations of the 20th century in the United States and would like to seriously pursue this work. Over the past several years, marketing researchers have assisted businesses by identifying specific characteristics of various generations (e.g., Baby Boomers, Generation X). A review of the literature, however, does not indicate that empirical studies have been conducted to substantiate these findings. I would like to establish a theoretical foundation for this area of research and design/conduct an empirical study of the differences in U.S. generations. I would also like to do some collaborative work studying generations across countries.

Other research interests include

- Developing best practices for breaking bad news. While some research in this area has been done, especially in the United Kingdom, it appears more work is needed to assist professionals who must break bad news including doctors, police officers, emergency room staff, and others. A review of the literature indicates few studies have been conducted in the United States, and professionals receive little training, if any, in this area.
- Studying why some minority cultures do not pursue higher educational opportunities while others do. For example, the Latino population is the fastest growing minority population in the United States, yet the numbers of Latinos attending U.S. colleges and universities do not appear to follow trends in population growth. One theory that does not appear to be discussed in the literature is worldview as it relates to access to higher education and retention of students. It would behoove higher education to study these issues from a cultural perspective in order to provide possible remedies.
- Researching human behavior in political environments. Although politics is about policy issues, it also appears to be even more about the art of persuasion, building relationships, and leadership characteristics. I believe this area would

make a fascinating study. In addition, a cursory review of colleges and universities indicates there are few, if any, programs to train individuals in developing success-ful political strategy.

My research interests have developed out of the areas of psychology to which I have been exposed. I seem to find areas of interest with each new experience.

Applicant D

My research interests fall generally within the domain of automatic cognitive processes that contribute to the development and maintenance of psychopathology. Much of this research incorporates theory from both the clinical and social cognition fields, and is grounded in the empirical investigation of processing along a continuum from normal to dysfunctional.

In particular, I am interested in the processing of threat-relevant information in anxiety disorders. In my dissertation work, in collaboration with Dr. Advisor, I am investigating the use of an implicit measure of cognitive processing as an assessment of automatic evaluations for individuals with XXX. The goal of the work is to extend evaluations of the cognitive model of anxiety by investigating implicit attitudes, which are automatic associations in memory that are somewhat analogous to schematic processing. I am evaluating whether this measure is sensitive to treatment effects and predictive of relapse (or return of fear). I am also investigating the relationship between different modalities of fear measurement, specifically, the synchrony between implicit pro-cesses, explicit questionnaires, behavioral self-report, and physiological measures of anxiety.

With this work, I hope to address a number of ambiguities in the anxiety literature. First, there has been no clear evaluation of implicit attitudes displayed by anxious subjects, despite substantial evidence that cognitive biases, such as selective attention, do exist for threat-related stimuli. Second, there is a lack of congruence between different modalities of fear responding, but little understanding of the mechanisms guiding the observed differences. The ultimate goal of this research is to add to our understanding of underlying cognitive schema in anxious individuals by more directly testing cognitive theories of anxiety than has previously been possible. If we can reliably predict automatic fear associations, this measure may potentially serve as either a prognostic indicator (i.e., a cognitive vulnerability marker), a measure of treatment progress, or as an index for those individuals who are at higher risk for relapse. Finally, looking at fearful implicit processing provides a unique opportunity to look at automatic attitudes in an emotion domain.

To further explore the malleability of automatic cognitive processes, I have been looking at implicit attitudes and beliefs toward obesity. Following from my work in eating disorders, I have been collaborating with Dr. Other Advisor to determine how manipulating both cognitive and affective information about obese individuals can augment or reduce implicit biases.

Additionally, to better understand the cognitive and affective dysregulation in psycho-pathology (anxiety in particular), Dr. Advisor and I recently completed a theoretical paper (Advisor & Me, 2000) outlining the role of disgust responding in anxiety disorders.

We evaluate the intersection of the related emotions, disgust and fear, in their range from normal to pathological to broaden our understanding of basic emotion, psychopathology, and treatment. Also, we have completed a study that empirically evaluates the relationship between disgust and fear, and the implications of this relationship with respect to exposure treatment for phobias.

Sample Responses to Question 5

5. How do you envision our internship site meeting your training goals and interests? (*Note:* This question requires you to address site-specific issues and training opportunities; thus, you may wish to submit different responses to different sites. If you are addressing these issues in a cover letter, please feel free to refer the reader to the cover letter and do not repeat here.)

Applicant A

I believe that the training philosophy of the ABC VA Medical Center predoctoral internship is consistent with my clinical interests and will help me meet my training goals for an internship. My primary training goal for internship is to continue my development as a scientist–practitioner. Thus, I am pursuing excellent clinical and research training within a Veteran Affairs Medical Center. I find that the quality and diversity of training, extensive supervision, and research experience offered by your internship site could be important to my development as a clinician, researcher, and teacher.

Your internship site also offers specific training opportunities consistent with my clinical interests and goals. I have spent a majority of my academic career obtaining expertise in diagnosis, assessment, and intervention strategies unique to those with dual diagnosis, trauma, and substance use. Consequently, I find the training offered at the posttraumatic stress disorder clinic and the substance abuse outpatient program rather attractive, as such training will allow me to continue developing and strengthening my clinical skills with these groups. I aspire to pursue a career dedicated to helping those with addictions and those with trauma histories through intervention and research. Thus, continued training in these areas will give me the experience and knowledge required for my long-term clinical and research goals. I have also found that your internship offers an opportunity to work at a Women's Health Center. Receiving training here would not only allow me to follow my passion for women's issues, but I would also have the possibility to receive even more training using the dialectical behavior therapy model. The opportunities at this particular center seem to be boundless and exciting. As someone who is committed to the scientist–practitioner model, I am also looking for an internship site that will allow me to continue to develop my identity as a researcher. One of my very long-term goals includes designing and empirically supporting a treatment for substance abusing trauma survivors. I would also like to investigate treatment utilization variables for these individuals. Therefore, I am excited about the opportunity to participate in a research team or to pursue my own supervised research project.

I am very impressed with the training offered at your internship site. Moreover, I believe that your internship's diverse training, scientist–practitioner philosophy,

PTSD, substance abuse, and women's center rotations, and research opportunities are consistent with my clinical interests, training needs, and long-term goals.

Applicant B

My long-term goal is a career in clinical research that provides opportunities to maintain an active role as a clinician, teacher, and supervisor. Toward this goal, I view internship as a valuable opportunity to build on the strong scientist–practitioner training I have received thus far. My primary training goals for internship are to (1) gain experience delivering evidence-based treatments for impulsive, aggressive, and self-injurious behaviors to more severely impaired populations than I have worked with previously; (2) enhance my skills for the evaluation and treatment of anxiety and depressive disorders in children and adolescents; and (3) enrich my understanding and proficiency with treatment models and modalities to which I have had more limited exposure (e.g., psychodynamic and family therapy).

I believe the child and adolescent internship program at the Site is the ideal internship site for me to meet these goals. The program emphasizes the use of an empirical approach to assessment and treatment in its training, supervision, and didactic courses, which is consistent with my scientist–practitioner training and with my desire to develop and evaluate effective treatments in the future. Along these lines, I am extremely interested in the opportunities to participate in the Site rotations at the Institute for the Study of Psychological Service and the Anxiety and Mood Disorders Service. The training offered in both of these clinics is consistent with my previous research and clinical experiences, as well as with my long-term career foci. I am also enthusiastic about the opportunities the program provides to work in the Child or Adolescent Inpatient Psychiatry Unit, as these rotations are also in line with my interest in working with individuals with more severe forms of psychopathology, particularly aggressive and self-injurious behaviors. Several other rotations, including the Pediatric Consultation Liaison Service and the adult forensic placements, are also of particular interest to me, and I look forward to learning more about these and other placements available to interns.

In most of my clinical experiences I have been trained in and have worked from a behavioral or cognitive–behavioral orientation. While I enjoy the flexibility and effectiveness of these approaches, I have also benefited from the range of experiences I have had working with supervisors from other perspectives, such as the psychodynamically oriented supervision I received on assessment and psychotherapy cases at the Practicum Rotation. I think it is crucial to my clinical training that I continue to gain exposure to a variety of assessment and treatment approaches, and I believe Site's commitment to using evidence-based evaluations and interventions, along with the diversity of clinical orientations and experiences offered, make your program an ideal site at which to accomplish my training goals.

From my experiences thus far, I have been fortunate to receive an excellent foundation of training in the theory, evaluation, and treatment of psychopathology. I believe the knowledge and expertise I have gained will help me be an active contributor to your internship program. Above all else, it is essential to me that I continue my training in a program that values the scientist–practitioner model and so successfully combines research and clinical practice. I am uniquely attracted to your internship program because I believe it will provide an excellent model for me as I embark on my career as a clinical researcher. Overall, my training in, and commitment to, evidence-based treatment and to research, combined with the range of clinical rotations and outstanding faculty that the child and adolescent internship program at the Site offers, make it an exceptional match for me.

Applicant C

While my experiences have provided me the opportunity to work with many diverse populations in a variety of different settings, I have found that working in an inpatient psychiatric setting is an excellent match for my interests, strengths, and abilities. My goal for this internship year is to gain supervised experience in the areas of psychological assessment and psychotherapy within an inpatient setting.

I would like to use this training year to further shape my professional identity. I have a strong interest in the General Adult Psychology rotation with its emphasis on psychological assessment, individual and group psychotherapy, and treatment planning. In addition, I would like to broaden my clinical focus to include forensic psychology. I have completed courses in this area but lack substantive experience. I am especially interested in learning to conduct forensic assessments, such as competency evaluations and risk assessments. I am also interested in learning to write opinions to the court as well as learning the skills necessary to be an effective expert witness. As a professional-in-training, I would like the opportunity to explore forensic psychology as a potential practice specialty. Although my exposure to neuropsychological assessment is limited, I would also welcome additional experience in this area, if possible.

I am looking for a site in which I can build upon my skills and abilities while learning and growing as a professional. I would welcome the opportunity to gain exposure to additional theoretical models of therapy, for example. While a cognitive–behavioral approach holds an intuitive appeal for me, I recognize the importance of acquiring training in other theoretical approaches for conducting individual and group therapy. I also have an interest in acquiring experience coleading or leading group therapy. Until now, my experience has focused on individuals or families, and I would like to broaden my focus to include group therapy.

One of my ongoing goals is to continue working with individuals of diverse backgrounds. I am a native from State X and envision I will continue to live and work in this region of the United States. The demographics of people living in State X are increasingly diverse. I recognize the importance of developing the skills necessary to work with people of diverse backgrounds and, at the same time, I enjoy working with people whose perspectives and worldviews differ from my own. I would like the opportunity to hone my skills in working with individuals of various races, cultural backgrounds, ages, sexual orientations, and spiritual beliefs.

The X State Hospital provides a number of opportunities that would address my training goals. In addition, the X State Hospital provides a unique opportunity to learn from psychologists in government service. I have worked over 15 years in X State government and understand many of the challenges this environment presents. I would appreciate the opportunity to work under the supervision of psychologists in government and hope to integrate this experience into my professional identity. I have experience working with complex issues in fast-paced environments and believe the X State Hospital would offer me the types of training and challenges I seek during my internship year. I am open to new experiences and I am eager to learn. I believe the X State Hospital is an excellent match for both my training and career goals.

Applicant D

I look forward to the opportunities provided during the internship year to build on my scientist–practitioner training. My short-term goals for internship include expanding my CBT skills and learning other evidence-based techniques to which I have had limited exposure. Along these lines, the chance to work with more severely ill clients than I have in the past is important to me, as well as broadening my experiences with minority populations. In many respects, X University is an ideal site for me to meet these immediate goals. First, the program emphasizes the application of basic experimental behavioral science to the understanding and treatment of adult behavior disorders, which fits with my scientist–practitioner training and University's mission to promote empirically validated treatments. Second, the opportunities to receive training in both the biological components of adult psychopathology and specialized instruction in treatment interventions that I have not practiced before, such as social skills group therapy, will allow me to expand my clinical expertise and skills. Third, the chance to work in one of the substance abuse programs or at the Women's Inpatient Treatment unit at Internship Hospital would allow me to gain exposure to new clinical populations. Also, given my clinical and research experience with anxiety disorders, I am enthusiastic about the possibilities for rotations outside the Adult Clinical area, such as Dr. Supervisor's program for children with anxiety problems and Dr. Supervisor's behavioral medicine rotation.

These new clinical opportunities build on my CBT training and provide new opportunities for me to continue my work integrating treatment and research. I am particularly interested in the possibility of building on my research looking at automatic processing in psychopathology and applying this work to the ongoing mood disorders grants at Internship. Furthermore, I look forward to learning about what kinds of collaborations would be possible on either the XXX Anxiety Research Project or the XXX Anxiety Disorders project.

With respect to my long-term objectives, I see the internship program at University preparing me for an academic career that has a strong scientific foundation. I view internship as a chance to develop as an evidence-based therapist and to learn how to mentor others in this model. The intensive year focused on clinical training will broaden my perspective on how treatment and research occur in diverse treatment settings. I want to make the most of this last opportunity for intense supervision at Internship, where I will be surrounded by innovative faculty and research and state-of-the-art clinical approaches. I feel that my commitment to evidence-based treatment and to research, combined with the range of clinical rotations and top research faculty that Internship offers make it an ideal match for me.

4 SUPPLEMENTARY MATERIALS

Carol Williams-Nickelson and Mitchell J. Prinstein

You have calculated your hours, completed your AAPI, and written thoughtful essays that truly reflect your training and career goals. The next step in the application process is to gather and write your supplementary materials, including your cover letter, your curriculum vitae (CV), and your letters of recommendation. Although it is rare, some sites may ask you to include a work sample, an additional essay question, or some other type of supplementary information to help them in their selection process. If this is the case, work with your director of clinical training (DCT) to determine which work sample should be included and how it should be presented to conceal the identity of the client, if relevant. Your DCT can also provide you with tips about how to answer additional essay questions. It is now uncommon for sites to ask for more information than what is included on the AAPI, but it is certainly possible, and these requests should be granted whenever possible.

Ultimately, the manner in which you prepare your supplementary materials will be based on your own professional style and personal preferences. Several examples of cover letters, CVs, and letters of recommendation have been provided in this chapter to offer some ideas. To help you prepare these documents, this chapter offers some guidelines regarding the purpose and most effective uses of your supplementary materials. Remember that your application folder will usually be reviewed in its entirety; thus, you will want all of your materials to fit together as a package that compellingly sells you as an intern applicant.

COVER LETTER

A cover letter is an introduction to you and your application packet, so it should not be a generic form letter. This is your first chance to set a tone and reveal some of your personality and professionalism through your writing style. Your cover letter provides a quick overview of your application packet and a nice opportunity to share personal information that may not otherwise fit within the AAPI or essays. Some argue that your cover letter may be the most important part of your application because it primes the reader for all else that follows. Therefore, your cover letter should be professional, typewritten, neat, organized, and well written. It should be printed on quality paper, like your CV, although remember that the content of your written materials is far more important than the type of paper on which it is printed. The cover letter should be brief (i.e., 1 page only, certainly no more than 2 pages). Keep in mind that reviewers of your application folder have many more pages of information to read and many more folders as well. Be succinct, concise, and clear.

A cover letter often begins with a paragraph indicating the name of the site or track to which you are applying, a list of materials included in the application packet, and a list of any additional materials that may arrive under separate cover. In subsequent paragraphs, the cover letter can offer a brief glimpse of the aspects of internship training that seem most relevant to your training goals. These paragraphs may briefly state an experience or set of experiences that have helped you to develop your training goals. Finally, a statement pertaining to the perceived match between you and the site may be appropriate (e.g., "The XX program is uniquely well matched to my training goals"), although remember that you are not permitted to provide any ranking information (e.g., "I will rank you number 1").

When writing the body of this letter, think of the text as an abstract of your application. In other words, make sure to highlight the main themes and points but do not restate any information that is explicitly listed within your AAPI or on your CV or offer new information that is not documented in the other materials. Thus, you should provide broad summary statements that tell the reader what you would like him or her to focus on when reviewing the rest of your application.

Finally, the cover letter may be an appropriate place to make the admissions committee aware of any personal reason you may have for relocation. This is certainly not required, but if you are looking for an opportunity to tell the committee that you must live in Montana next year, then this may be the place to do it. Or, you may wish to just let the committee know that you would seriously consider relocation (e.g., "I am looking forward to the possibility of moving to Honolulu") to convey your serious interest in the site. This may be especially important for programs that are in less-desirable locations and want to ensure that applicants are seriously interested in their site.

You may also decide to include something personal in your cover letter to give the reviewers a sense of who you are. Many training directors may appreciate this approach or respect your candor and authenticity. However, others may feel that personal disclosures are inappropriate and indicative of loose boundaries. It is best to share personal information only if you are comfortable doing so, if this decision feels most congruent with who you are, and if you feel that this information is essential to communicate when applying for internship training.

In summary here are some helpful cover letter tips:

- Tailor your cover letter to the site, and call attention to specific information on your AAPI and CV that match particularly well with the site.
- Do not introduce new information in the cover letter.
- Refrain from sending a generic or standardized cover letter.
- Show you are interested enough in the site to do your homework. Direct the letter to the correct person and double-check, even triple-check, for spelling accuracy. Also include a comment about training opportunities and characteris-

tics of the site that you really like, as well as your enthusiasm for their unique program.

Several examples of cover letters that you may find useful are at the end of this chapter.

Internship sites expect that you will submit a CV with your application and not a résumé. A résumé is a concise snapshot of you and your qualifications for a particular job. A CV is more comprehensive and can be thought of as an evolving document. Keep in mind that your CV is a tool to inform and persuade; thus, it should be written in a compelling, accurate manner. The CV is also a reflection of who you are. Hence, you want to be sure that it is error free and easy to read and understand.

You should write your CV with a particular professional audience in mind. In this case, your audience includes internship training directors and faculty. Therefore, you should try to emphasize your clinical experiences and competencies but also be economical with your use of words; be consistent with your style, grammar, and tense; use an active voice; and know that it is permissible to use psychological jargon. A sloppy CV may be indicative of a sloppy clinician. A CV with excessive use of fonts, underlines, and graphics may be more helpful when applying for a job in computer science than in psychology.

Some people include a lot of personal information on their CVs, including photographs. Certainly, this is a stylistic decision, but we recommend that you not include a picture, your date of birth, the number of children you have, your height and weight, your hobbies, your astrological sign, or similar items. These inclusions are likely to be interpreted as offering too much information or as "padding" your CV with unnecessary material. Other common but questionable text includes information about where you attended high school, that you were the captain of your college football team, or that you won a beauty contest when you were an undergraduate. Although some training directors may be very interested in hearing about these things, we think that it is better to save this personal information for a conversation rather than as activities to highlight on your CV.

Other examples of padding your CV may include class presentations, the names of conferences you attended, published abstracts in addition to a duplicate list of presentations, and so forth. Most sites will ask for a transcript that already documents your coursework. Unless you have a specific purpose for including class presentations or naming the conferences you attended, it may be best to leave these off of your CV. If, on the other hand, you attended a special seminar or workshop and became certified to facilitate a particular type of training or education program that is relevant, it would be perfectly appropriate to include that information. Finally, as with everything else, give your CV to others to review.

Usually, a desire to create a lengthy CV originates from a concern that one has too few accomplishments or may be evaluated as underqualified. Remember that you are applying for a training position; thus, you need to demonstrate that you are "trainable," which does not necessarily mean that you need to be fully competent yet. If the DCT in your graduate program says that you are ready to apply for internship, then you probably are!

Constructing Your CV

The following list of Do's and Don'ts for constructing your CV offers overarching strategies that will help you develop a CV that is effective in presenting your experiences and skills in a professional manner while reflecting your personality.

- *Do* know the difference between a résumé and a CV. You should submit a CV with your internship application. A *résumé* is a concise, business-style report that displays your job qualifications to a prospective employer. It is usually 2–3 pages long; reflects basic information about education, work experience, volunteerism, awards, and publications; includes a statement of goals, purpose, or objectives; and lists specific skills, achievements, and education and training accomplishments that make you a likely candidate for a specific job. It is a snapshot of your employment experience. On the other hand, a *CV* is unlimited in length and is an evolving document that includes information covered on a résumé, without the statement of goals, purpose, or objectives. A CV records more descriptive information about education, training, work experience, volunteerism, awards, publications, presentations, demonstration of leadership or professional service, research, and the like. It is a comprehensive picture of you. Interestingly, *curriculum vitae* is Latin for the "course of (one's) life."
- *Do* understand that you will probably have to edit several drafts of your CV to make it clearer, more concise, and increasingly polished. Even though your CV is endlessly perfectible, *don't* require yourself to create a perfect document.
- *Do* avoid jargon and slang, but *don't* confuse precise technical language (i.e., the specialized language psychologists use) with jargon. Precise technical language is the shortest, clearest, and most appropriate way to communicate within our profession, and it is fine to use this language in your CV.
- *Do* remember that the purpose of your CV is to inform and persuade.
- *Do* tell your CV reader what he or she needs to know, and place information in an order that is most useful to them.
- *Do* think about the audience for which you are preparing your CV. For example, consider the type of site to which you are applying (e.g., counseling center, Veterans Administration, medical center). How much does your audience know about your experiences (i.e., your program, your practica, your work experience, your professional involvement)? What questions can you anticipate from your audience (and address in your CV)? Have you omitted any significant information that the audience needs?
- *Do* remember that depending on experience, education, mindsets, and conceptual frameworks, every CV reader will react differently to the same words on a page, and you will not have complete control over audience responses.
- *Do* present the facts without distortion.
- *Do* remember that an economy of words is desirable; complete sentences are not necessary.
- *Do* use lists whenever appropriate.
- *Do* use topic headings to increase organization and ease of readability.
- *Do* use consistent grammatical structures. If you begin with active verbs, continue to use active verbs throughout. Pay attention to verb tense across experi-

ences, and *don't* mix tenses. If you begin with complete sentences instead of sentence fragments, use complete sentences throughout.

- *Don't* include your date or place of birth, height and weight, health condition, relationship status, hobbies or interests, religion, type of automobile you drive, favorite color, astrological sign, or similar information. Remember, this is a document to help you gain a professional position, not to help you find a date or new social group.

- *Don't* provide information because you *can* provide it—it may be unnecessary and even unhelpful (e.g., name of high school, elementary school penmanship awards, cheerleading experience, previous modeling career, star of your community basketball team). Inclusion of this information is certainly your choice, but think about the possible interpretations and implications of those interpretations.

- *Don't* include a picture.

- *Do* tactfully acknowledge your skills by describing what you have done and what you do rather than using broad and vague adjectives or pretentious, obscure, and esoteric language. For example, the words *responsible, intelligent,* and *committed* are too vague. Describe how you have been responsible. Offer information that will help the reader see that you are intelligent. Discuss projects or activities you have been involved with and seen through to the end to demonstrate commitment. As another example, referring to the act of smelling something as "olfactory analysis" is unnecessarily obscure. Be vivid and precise.

- *Do* use active versus passive voice.

- *Do* remember that your CV is your written portrait. Like your personal appearance in a face-to-face interview, the physical appearance, or format, of your CV is important, testifying to your initiative, ability to communicate, and overall professionalism. It helps people know what you have to offer; it is an extension of you. Your personality and work style will be judged by the presentation of your CV.

- *Do* make yourself memorable by the overall quality and content of your CV.

Organizing Your CV

The information on your CV should be organized into logical groupings. Following is an outline and discussion of the major areas of the CV in a natural progressive order of information.

1. **Name, Address, Telephone and Fax Number(s) With Area Code, and E-mail Address**
   - Position this information at the top of the first page.
   - Place last name and page number at the top or bottom of every additional page.
   - Use a permanent address and telephone number; you may list both a home and a work number.
2. **Goals, Purpose, or Objectives**
   - Do not include this information on a CV.
3. **Personal or Demographic Information**
   - Be very cautious and deliberate with what you reveal.

4. Education
- List the entries in chronological order.
- List the name, location (city, state), area code and telephone number, degree earned, graduation date, major(s), cumulative GPAs (optional), and GPAs in major (optional) for each university and degree.
- List honors, scholarships, and awards either with each institution or under a separate category.
- Do not include high school, as it is probably not necessary.
- Include information about a degree (undergraduate or graduate) in an interesting or allied profession if you wish.

5. Employment (if applicable)
- List entries in chronological order, starting with the most recent job first.
- Include name, mailing address (including zip code), area code and telephone number, and the name of your last supervisor with his or her title and degree.
- Do *not* report salary information.
- List the last position or job title you held.
- List your dates of employment from month/year to month/year.
- Include a narrative or bulleted points that describe your specific duties, including workload, type of work, level of responsibility, supervision provided to others, programs developed or administered, special projects, achievements, promotions, positions held that led to current position, and any budgetary responsibilities (use active voice and avoid vague adjectives).
- Include work awards and commendations.
- Do *not* include your reason for leaving the position.

Example:

PacifiCare, Inc.   Oct 1997–Present
567 Insurance Drive   *Supervisor:* Martin Evil, MBA
Somewhere North, CA 90745
(915) 879-6688

Position: Claims Reviewer and Authorizer

Responsibilities: Provide consultation to physicians in developing insurance-approved treatment plans; authorize laboratory work and medical testing based on insurer's benefit plan and medical need; complete quarterly cost–benefit analyses; and specialize in behavioral health services.

6. Volunteer or Service Work
- Format this section similar to the employment section with name, mailing address, area code and telephone number, supervisor or volunteer coordinator, and dates of service.
- Include an official title, if applicable.
- Report responsibilities.

7. Practica or Psychotherapy Experience
- Format this section similar to the employment and volunteer sections.
- Include the names of all supervisors.

- Specify type of services, population served, special treatment protocol and interventions used, amount of testing, consultation, multidisciplinary team work, average time spent weekly or monthly at the site, range of presenting problems, psychotropic medication management, and other services provided.

Example:

Friendly Medical Center   Sept 1996–Present
Department of Behavioral Medicine   *Supervisor:*
Behavioral Health   Sandy Stressfree, PhD
888 Bypass Rd.
Somewhere North, CA 90745

Responsibilities: Provide health psychology services to a range of patients suffering from cognitive impairment, high blood pressure, chronic pain, and depression; complete neuropsychological assessments; provide individual and group therapy to patients and their family members; work as part of an interdisciplinary team with psychiatrists, physicians, nurses, social workers, and rehabilitation therapists in the urology, cardiac, surgical recovery and orthopedic departments; use hypnotherapy and cognitive–behavioral therapy interventions; conduct standardized smoking cessation programs; and participate in grand rounds.

Hours: Approximately 20 hours per week at hospital (16 hours direct service and consultation, 4 hours administrative duties and test interpretation).

Cumulative Practica Hours: 187 direct service hours, 46 administrative hours.

8. **Provision of Supervision (optional)**
   - Describe your supervisory experience and style.
   - Describe the type of supervision offered (i.e., live, group, individual, video- or audiotaped).
   - List supervisee characteristics (i.e., provided supervision to social workers, master's counseling students; primarily supervised couples therapy cases).
9. **Professional Affiliations and Leadership Roles**
   - List all memberships in professional associations.
   - List level of membership (e.g., affiliate, student, associate, full) and make sure you are documenting this correctly.
   - Indicate membership duration.
   - Describe the professional organization if is it not commonly known.
   - List any offices, roles, or projects associated with professional organization membership or involvement.
   - List special committee memberships (e.g., advisory board, steering committee, school senate).
10. **Awards and Scholarships**
    - List the name of the award or scholarship, who nominated, who bestowed, type of award or scholarship, and date conferred. (There are very few universally recognized and understood awards and scholarships, so you need to describe what you won and why you won it.)

- Indicate dollar amounts for awards or scholarships if they are substantial or provide important information.

11. **Licensure**
    - Include any licenses you hold, the name of the licensing board, and your license number.

12. **Teaching Experience**
    - List the name of university, department, mailing address, dates of teaching, and supervisor(s) names in a format similar to the employment listings.
    - Indicate the name and level of the course(s) you taught and the number of times each course was taught at each institution.

13. **Research**
    - List your research projects as well as your dissertation research.
    - Include details about the nature of your research involvement. (Do you run subjects, analyze data, train research assistants to administer particular assessments?)
    - Include the names of your research supervisor(s), dissertation chair, and purpose of the research (i.e., research assistant, significant class project).

14. **Grants**
    - List the title of the project, name of the funding agency, and dates of the funding.
    - List your role on the grant (PI, Co-PI; Co-I, Consultant).
    - Include the dollar amount of the grant (optional).

15. **Professional Presentations**
    - List presentations at professional conferences and workshops.
    - Use the most recent APA style for referencing.

16. **Publications**
    - List any publications and manuscripts in print, in press, under review, and (perhaps) in preparation.
    - Use the most recent APA style for referencing.
    - List only articles in professional publications (i.e., not in the school newspaper or supermarket circular unless you have a deliberate reason for doing so).

17. **Other Sections (if applicable)**
    - Do not list continuing education workshops that you have attended or special presentations that you have attended at national, state, or local conferences, as most CV reviewers do not find this information useful or enhancing. In fact, it can be interpreted as padding your CV thus could detract from your substantive work.
    - List conferences attended only if you have a specific reason (e.g., to document specialty training) for including this information (and make that reason clear to the reviewer).
    - List special courses only if you have a specific reason (e.g., to document unique certification of skills) for including this information (and make that reason clear to the reviewer). Your internship site will usually have your transcripts, and if they do not ask for your transcripts to be included with your application materials, they generally are not interested in reviewing a list of your classes. Thus, you should not include such a list on your CV.

18. References

- Be sure to check with references before providing their names and contact information to others, and try to alert them of any potential calls ahead of time.
- Give your references your CV and other information to make it easy for them to highlight your outstanding accomplishments.

Several examples of CVs are provided at the end of this chapter.

LETTERS OF RECOMMENDATION

Most applicants can secure positive letters of recommendation that attest to clinical competence and internship readiness. This is expected. However, what sets your recommendation letters apart from other letters is evidence of the following:

1. You are genuinely liked and respected by your peers, faculty, and supervisors.
2. You consistently demonstrate professionalism.
3. You can work well with others—your peers, your supervisors, and your subordinates. You are collegial and respectful.
4. You are committed to learning; even though you may enter the internship with impressive skills, you are interested in expanding those skills.
5. You are responsible, responsive, and hard-working, and you complete high-quality work.
6. You are a leader.
7. You are invested in the profession.
8. You are *normal*.

Your goal is to obtain recommendation letters that offer the most accurate and positive description of your skills, accomplishments, and personal demeanor. When you ask someone for a letter, specifically ask, "Can you write a *strong* letter of support?" If they answer "yes" without hesitation, then you can assume that their letter will be helpful. If they express any reservation, you should ask someone else.

Applicants often wonder about strategies for gathering recommendation letters from particular psychologists. They ask, "What if two of my supervisors from the same practicum site write me letters? Does this make it seem like my other practica supervisors cannot write strong letters?" "What if all of my letters are from junior faculty?" "Will it increase my chances of being ranked high if I have 'high-profile' psychologists write my letters?"

Our advice is that you try not to worry about any other strategy except getting strong letters from people who know you and your work very well. Oftentimes, the "high-profile psychologist" letters do not impress internship sites, unless these psychologists can speak in-depth about your clinical and personal skills. If you have the choice between sending a weak letter from a "big-name" psychologist versus a very strong letter from a junior faculty member, we recommend that you ask the junior faculty member to write the letter.

Some people also wonder whether it is advisable to solicit a letter of recommendation from a nonpsychologist (e.g., a physician, psychiatrist, social worker). Although these referees may be able to comment on your ability to work within a multidisciplinary setting, it is less likely that these professionals will be able to comment on the types of skills and competencies that are expected of doctoral-level psychologists, and therefore, it may be better to obtain letters exclusively from psychologists.

You should begin cultivating relationships with potential letter writers now. Make appointments to talk with your advisor, supervisors, and other faculty members whom you might ask to write letters. During your meetings with these psychologists, tell them about yourself. Tell them that you are trying to get to know more about him or her and vice versa. Provide the psychologist with a copy of your CV. Discuss your research ideas. Discuss your practica experiences. Tell him or her about your previous jobs, volunteer work, and leadership activities. Most important, tell him or her about your goals for training on internship. In short, give these psychologists information about yourself that will help them form an accurate and comprehensive professional and personal opinion of you so that they will have the necessary information to write a strong recommendation letter when the time comes.

To review, here are a couple of recommendation letter rules to remember:

1. Ask psychologists (people with doctorate degrees in psychology) to write recommendation letters for you. You are applying to a pre*doctoral* internship. More often than not, reviewers will value letters from their psychologist–colleagues more than letters from allied professionals, such as social workers, marriage/ family therapists, or psychiatrists. (If, however, you are applying to a site where working collaboratively with psychiatrists is a large part of the internship, it might be appropriate to have a strong letter of support submitted by a psychiatrist. Use your best judgment here.)
2. Ask the writers of your recommendation letters if they would like you to provide them with pre-stamped and pre-addressed envelopes. This helps to make the task as simple as possible for your recommenders.
3. Give your letter writers sufficient time to compose and send the letters. Do not expect them to respond to your urgency. If there are different deadlines for your recommendation letters, you may want to order your pre-stamped/pre-addressed envelopes according to the deadlines and put a stick-it note on the envelope with a "please mail by" date.

SUMMARY

The supplementary materials that you will submit with your AAPI include a cover letter, CV, recommendation letters, and any unique materials that are site specific. Together, these materials will convey your experience, interests, professionalism, and perhaps also some of your personal characteristics. Now that you have prepared your applications, mailed them to the sites, and received calls to set up interviews, it is time to rest. In only a few weeks, you should start hearing from sites about interviews— the subject of the next chapter.

Sample Cover Letter 1

Date

Dr. XXX
Address
City, State, and Zip

Dear Dr. XXX,

I am a fourth-year graduate student in clinical child/family psychology at the University of XXX. I would like to apply for the internship program at the XXX for the 2001–2002 year. I have enclosed the required application materials, as outlined in your program brochure, which includes the APPIC uniform application, a copy of my curriculum vitae, a graduate transcript from the University of XXX (for which an official copy has also been mailed under a separate cover), and a self-addressed postcard. Four letters of recommendation from Drs. A, B, C, and D have been mailed to you directly.

I am strongly and uniquely interested in the XXX internship program and the opportunity to continue my training in clinical child psychology. Primarily, I am drawn to your program to increase my exposure to the presentation of severe psychopathology in children while working with supervisors representing a range of disciplines and orientations. I am also very interested in the opportunity to gain more experience in family therapy. In addition, the chance to continue my work with ethnically and financially diverse clients at XXX offers an excellent match to one of my primary internship goals.

I am also very excited about the possibility of relocating to X-city. I had the opportunity to visit X-city in (year) to attend the XXX conference, and I greatly enjoyed my stay. I have several close friends in the X-city area who have long raved about the pleasures of living there.

Thank you for considering my application to your internship program, and I look forward to hearing from you.

Sincerely,

Your Name

Date

Predoctoral Internship Admissions Committee
XXX University

Dear Dr. X,

Enclosed please find my application for the Predoctoral Internship Program at XXX (Child Clinical–Pediatric track). As requested, I have included a copy of the APPIC application form, current curriculum vitae, graduate school transcript, and three signed/sealed letters of reference. Please note that, on my graduate transcript, the titles of the courses I have taken may be unclear, therefore I am also including a separate sheet that lists the full course titles.

Your internship program has been recommended to me as an excellent training site in pediatric and child clinical psychology by a number of psychologists and colleagues, including Dr. XXX and Dr. XXX, both of whom have been consulting with me on my dissertation research. I have spoken with Dr. XXX, one of your former interns, who was incredibly positive about his internship experience at XXX. After reading through your application materials, I was pleased to see how closely your program matches my particular set of internship goals and interests. I have a very strong interest in pediatric and child clinical psychology and, as detailed on my application, I feel that your internship would be an ideal place for me to further develop and broaden my clinical skills and abilities.

I am very excited about your internship and believe that I would be a good match to your program. I would be very happy to meet with you and your colleagues, at your convenience, to discuss my application as well as your program's training opportunities.

Should you have any questions about my application, I can be reached at home at XXX, in the lab at XXX, or by email at XXX. I look forward to hearing from you.

Sincerely,

Your Name

Sample Cover Letter 3

Date

Dear Training Director,

I am extremely interested in the Geriatric Subtrack of the Internship Program at X. My clinical and research interests, as well as my career goals, are in geriatric psychopathology. Clinically, I have worked for 2 years on a medical/psychiatric unit at X Hospital with Dr. XX, and I am currently externing at X Hospital with Dr. YY. At these settings, I have grown to appreciate and value the unique challenges of the geriatric psychology populations.

I have also worked on various research projects in this area, including identifying optimal reinforcement schedules for elders with dementia, investigating medical and dietary compliance issues for elders diagnosed with diabetes, and administering the Dementia Rating Scale to assess changes in intellectual functioning of elderly with renal failure following dialysis. During my graduate training, I have been under the supervision of Dr. XX. My thesis project involved the evaluation of distress levels of elderly individuals with dementia during dialysis treatments. My work in this area was distinguished by the XXX Award from the Association of X. I believe that my experience and training will allow me to benefit from and contribute to your program in substantial ways.

I am excited about the possibility of moving to State, USA. I believe this location will be a nice place to continue my career.

Please find enclosed the APPIC uniform application, personal statement, supplemental information form, curriculum vitae, and a stamped, self-addressed postcard.

I look forward to hearing from you.

Regards,

Your Name

Sample Curriculum Vitae 1

CAMILE CHAMELEON

HOME	**OFFICE**
The Street, Apt. C	University of Psychology
My City, Illinois 46545	Counseling Center
(222) 222-4444 Phone/Fax	300 Health Services Bldg.
	My City, Illinois 46556
Email: CamileWestfield.54@sphs.edu	(222) 555-5555

EDUCATION

My University   Aug 1993–Present
Friendliness, Texas
    Doctoral Student in APA-Accredited Counseling
    Psychology Program
    PsyD Candidate for August 2000 Graduation
    Master of Science in Counseling Psychology   Aug 1995
        Specialization in Marriage & Family Therapy

University of Provo   Feb 1986–Aug 1989
Provo, Utah
    Bachelor of Science   Aug 1989
    ■ *Major: Psychology*
    ■ *Minor: Sociology*

EMPLOYMENT

Nursing Home Social Service Consultant   June 1993–June 1999
Self-employed
Friendliness, Texas
Position: Social Service Consultant
Responsibilities: Provided consultation to staff and Social Service Directors (SSDs) working with elderly residents and their families; reviewed and supervised social service treatment planning; provided consultation to address resident behavioral and affective problems; completed psychosocial assessments and psychosocial histories/ evaluations; made recommendations for interventions; conducted staff trainings; designed programs for dementia care units; interviewed, hired, and trained SSDs; evaluated SSD performance and compliance with state standards; facilitated elderly and caregiver groups.

Support Health Services, Inc.   Feb 1997–July 2000
Post Office Box 781296
Friendliness, Texas
Position: Director
Responsibilities: Directed all operations for company that provided medical personnel staffing on a contractual basis in a variety of hospital and clinical settings; supervised and hired all management, executive, and line staff; authored service contracts.

Friendliness Police Department
Psychological Services
3635 East Houston—Eastside Substation
Friendliness, Texas
Position: Crisis Response Team Counselor

Sept 1996–Feb 1997
Supervisors: Paul Smith,
PhD & Martha
Stewart, PhD

Responsibilities: Worked in tandem with uniformed police officer responding to police emergency calls involving domestic disturbance/violence and crisis-related incidents to provide immediate mental health intervention; brief counseling; worked with court system to obtain protective orders, issue warrants & file charges; victim's advocacy; conducted officer trainings; community outreach; community presentations; collaborated with other units within the police department including homicide, family violence, and sexual assault.

Manor Health Care
(Four Seasons Nursing Center)
8300 W Street
Friendliness, Texas 78229
Position: Director of Social Services

July 1993–Sept 1996
Supervisor: Darren Star,
Administrator

Responsibilities: Management/Clinical position responsible for psychosocial needs of 151 residents affected with Alzheimer's Disease and other dementias; coordinated and led interdisciplinary treatment planning process; discharge planning; conducted support groups for residents and families; completed social histories and psychosocial evaluations; advocated for resident rights; monitored the use of physical restraints and psychotropic medication use and provided related education to family and staff regarding its use and effects; introduced behavior modification programs; conducted staff trainings; coordinated adjunct psychological and family therapy services; supervised juvenile community service restitution program for adolescents completing community service hours; community seminars; coordinated facility continuous quality improvement program.

Life Management Center for
Mental Health/Mental Retardation
8929 Viscount Blvd.
El Paso, Texas 79990
Position: Social Worker

Dec 1992–Feb 1993
Supervisor: Melvin
Carrison, LMSW

Responsibilities: Worked with chronically mentally ill adults on the SANAR unit (Screening, Assessment, Networking, Advocacy, and Referral); completed intake evaluations and placed clients in appropriate follow-up mental health programs; participated in treatment planning with psychiatry interns; assisted with state hospital commitments; acted as a liaison in transferring state hospital clients into outpatient programs; provided crisis counseling and intervention.

Inland Counties Regional Center
1020 Cooley Drive
Colton, California 92324
Position: Social Worker III

May 1992–Sept 1992
Supervisor: Patrick
Hammond, MS

Responsibilities: Provided case management services for transition-aged developmentally disabled population; completed quarterly and annual reviews of clients to include the CDER diagnostic evaluation; completed annual Individual Program Plans; advocated for client's educational and employment opportunities/rights; participated in Individual Education Plan meetings; arranged client placement in residential treatment facilities; completed facility audits; maintained a case load of 90 clients.

Inland Behavioral Services, Inc.   Sept 1989–Sept 1992
1963 North "E" Street   Supervisor: Ed Wilson,
Jackson, California 92405   LMSW
Position: Outpatient Clinic Director/Substance Abuse Counselor
Responsibilities: Managed outpatient drug and alcohol counseling clinic servicing all ages; supervised 10 counselors; conducted individual and group counseling sessions; hired and trained all substance abuse counselors; developed and implemented "Teen Advantage" program for adolescents at risk for substance abuse, gang membership and incarceration which is now used throughout the Los Angeles and Jackson County school districts, probation departments, and juvenile detention centers; completed monthly statistical reports for submission to county and federal govt.; served on the School Advisory and Review Board; collaborated with parole, probation, and protective service agencies; responsible for the delivery of services for the Calif. Penal Code 1000 first-time drug offender program; completed treatment plans and progress notes; counselor for the Jackson County Juvenile Detention Center's female unit (primarily female gang members); consultant, program developer, counselor and outreach worker for the Mayor's drug and gang task force in Los Angeles; prevention counseling for identified gang members in the juvenile detention centers; crisis counseling.

Olive Crest Treatment Centers   Sept 1990–Apr 1991
25809 Business Center Drive   Supervisor: Dottie
Redlands, California 92374   Ethridge, LMSW
Position: Caseworker II
Responsibilities: Case management for adolescent male sex offenders; supervised client's recreational therapy program; controlled and administered psychotropic medications; participated in treatment team meetings and treatment plan development; completed daily progress notes; implemented level system; crisis counseling.

Inland Empire Residential Treatment   Sept 1990–Apr 1991
710 Church Street   Supervisor: Beth
Redlands, California 92374   Whimpt, MS
Position: Counselor
Responsibilities: Counseled mentally ill male children ages 4 to 10 with histories of physical and sexual abuse; controlled and administered psychotropic medication; implemented behavioral incentive program; supervised parental visits; daily behavioral management; trained in the use of noninjurious restraint methods; crisis counseling and intervention.

Optimist Boys' Home and Ranch   Sept 1989–Sept 1990
South Bay Group Home   Supervisor: Ben Savage,
6957 North Figueora   PhD
Los Angeles, California
Position: Counselor II

Responsibilities: Counseled male adolescents identified as known gang members on probation residing in an emancipation group home as well as those living at the main campus/facility in Los Angeles; facilitated prevention and rehabilitation program to mandated youth attending outpatient gang diversion program; collaborated with inter-disciplinary team for court recommendations for adolescent's incarceration in the California Youth Authority; approved/denied all parental visits and home passes based upon parental interviews; facilitated social skills groups in the group homes; controlled and administered psychotropic medications; maintained clinical records; designed dis-cipline protocol; participated in treatment team meetings and treatment plan develop-ment; discharge planning; acted as liaison between probation officers, social workers, and clients.

VOLUNTEER WORK

The University of Psychology   Aug 1999–Present
Office of Multicultural Student Affairs
Mentored an ethnic-minority freshman woman to help ensure success and comfort as a new college student in a highly competitive academic environment.

Fisher House, Inc.   Apr 1996–June 1999
Salvation Medical Center
Army Air Force Base
Friendliness, Texas
Family Friends program developer and trainer; wrote volunteer training and continuing education program used to train new volunteers to work with families of bone marrow transplant recipients; conducted ongoing in-services and skill development seminars; served on Advisory Board for the Fisher House at Army AFB.

United Way Teen Helpline Evaluation Committee   June 1996–Aug 1996
Friendliness, Texas
Member of committee composed of professionals with expertise in working with teens in crisis to evaluate the functioning of the Teen Helpline and make recommendations regarding the future of the Teen Helpline.

Association for Death Education and Counseling   Apr 1996–June 1999
Hartford, CT
Member of the student Executive Committee as the Membership Coordinator; volun-teer worker at the 1996 annual conference in Pittsburgh.

Transplants for Children   Feb 1996–June 1999
Friendliness, Texas
Facilitator for monthly couples group composed of parents of children waiting for organs to become available for transplants.

United Way Helpline   Aug 1995–June 1999
Friendliness, Texas
Position: Clinical Backup. Responded to Helpline volunteers when they have difficulty managing crisis calls—i.e., their caller is in danger and refuses to disclose their location; provided online crisis counseling; gave volunteers authorization to trace high risk calls;

assessed suicide lethality and decided on the type of intervention warranted in each case; coached the volunteer.

Texas Psychological Association   Sept 1994–Nov 1995
Austin, Texas
Member of the Planning Committee for the 1995 Annual Convention as well as chair/coordinator of the volunteer committee; Employment Network Chair (recruited and organized job placement at the convention).

Senior Olympics   March 1994, Apr 1995,
Friendliness, Texas   July 1996
Event coordinator, Senior citizen sponsor.

Volunteers in Probation (V.I.P.)   April 1991–Sept 1992
San Bernardino, California
Conducted drug and gang prevention groups in the juvenile detention facility.

Jackson County Community Against Drugs   April 1991–Sept 1992
Jackson, California
Participated in organizing various youth activities, including Red Ribbon Week, to keep adolescents off the streets and educated about the consequences of drug use and gang membership.

PROFESSIONAL AFFILIATIONS

American Psychological Association (1993–present)—Student member APA Divisions 12, 17, 20, 31, & 43; Affiliate—American Psychological Association Divisions of Clinical Psychology, Counseling Psychology, Adult Development and Aging, State Psychological Associations, and Family Psychology

Texas Psychological Association (1993–present)—Student member
Texas Psychological Association: Division of Students in Psychology—Student Member

Bexar County (Texas) Psychological Association (1993–present)—Student member

My City Psychological Association (1999–present)—Student member

American Association for Marriage and Family Therapy (1993–1999)—Student member

Friendliness Association for Marriage and Family Therapy (1993–1999)—Student member

National Association of Social Workers (1993–present)—Member

Association for Death Education and Counseling (1994–present)—Associate Member

OFFICES/POSITIONS HELD WITHIN THE PROFESSIONAL ORGANIZATIONS:

APAGS-Advocacy Coordinating Team Subcommittee—APAGS Campus Representative (10–93 to 10–97)
Represented APAGS on campus to psychology students and served as mediator to relay student concerns, questions, and issues to the APAGS Board for consideration; kept students abreast of professional and legislative issues as directed by APAGS.

Bexar County Psychological Association, Executive Committee Student Ex-Officio Member (10–93 to 08–99)
Attended BCPA Board meetings to represent student perspectives and interests for event planning and general policy purposes.

Bexar County Psychological Association, Student Advocacy Committee Chair (10–93 to 08–99)
Led the student membership of BCPA in advocating for student inclusion in various BCPA activities; responsible for the organization and implementation of two "Psychology and Mental Health Providers Career and Networking Fairs" sponsored by BCPA, tailored to introduce students to psychology job opportunities and careers in Bexar County as well as assist psychologists in securing or changing jobs; organized two "Resume Writing and Interview Skills" workshops for students and psychologists in preparation for the fairs.

University of Psychology—Psychology Graduate Student Association (08–93 to 06–99)
Student representative for the Marriage & Family Therapy program and Professional Counseling program (Dual Tract) while a Master's student (08–93 to 08–95). Doctoral Student Representative on the Council (08–95 to 06–99). Elected President of the student association for six consecutive years (08–93 to 06–99). Participated in Master's program, Doctoral program, and faculty interviewing processes; served as liaison between students and faculty/administration; developed departmental newsletter; created and led biannual student forums; organized and offered monthly workshops and brown-bag seminars related to special topics and professional issues.

ADVISORY BOARDS/COMMITTEES

The Zachary and Elizabeth M. Fisher House, Inc.   April 1997–June 1999
Advisory Board Member
Participated in ongoing decision-making processes related to this program that provides housing and emotional support/counseling to families of active duty and retired military personnel as they await organ transplants.

TEACHING

The University of Psychology	Fall 1999–Present
Lecturer/Instructor–Psychology Department	Supervisor: Bill Clinton,
Courses taught:	PhD
Abnormal Psychology (*1 time*)	
The University of the Other One	Fall 1996–Summer 1999
Part-Time Instructor—Psychology Department	Supervisor: Don King,
Courses taught:	PhD
Introduction to Psychology (*4 times*)	

RESEARCH

Extra-Sensory Perception   June 1997–Present
Dissertation research examining ESP, stress, and expectations among those with special powers.

The University of Psychology Health Science Center   Feb 1997–Sept 1997

Research Assistant to Den Pen, MD, medical school faculty member and researcher. Involved in a partner abuse study and facilitated focus groups for women; completed work on qualitative analysis of the focus group narratives.

Couples Therapy in Violent Relationships   Sept 1996–Feb 1997

Assisted in research project through the Friendliness Police Department on the efficacy of systemic therapy vs. individual therapy with violent couples using quantitative and qualitative measures.

Crisis Intervention Assessment   Nov 1996–Jan 1997

Participated in developing an assessment tool for police officer use in crisis (violent) situations to assess lethality (Friendliness Police Department).

Domestic Violence and Women   Feb 1996–Nov 1996

Investigated women's perceptions of violence in our culture and the way they make meaning and define violence within their own lives; qualitative data analysis used to code transcripts from interviews conducted with women from various settings who were self-identified or identified by others as victims of violent acts as part of a doctoral course.

Friendliness Police Officers Association   Oct 1995–Feb 1997

Completed research tasks on special interest areas related to police officers and mental health, in conjunction with Detective Jim Jones. Used special gifts—particularly ESP—to locate criminals for the police department.

LICENSURE

National Association of Social Workers—Social Work Associate, License 123456

AWARDS AND SCHOLARSHIPS

Texas Psychological Association   Nov 1998

Recipient of the 1998 "Advancing the Science of Psychology through Serving the Students" Award.

My University—Service Award   1997–1998

Recipient of the 1997–1998 University Service Award "in recognition and appreciation for your valuable gifts of time and talent for the benefit of the entire University."

My University—Service Award   1995–1996

Recipient of the 1995–1996 University Service Award (same as previous).

Association for Death Education and Counseling   Spring 1996

Recipient of the 1996 Student Initiative Scholarship.

American Association of University Women   August 1995

Recipient of the 1995 AAUW Scholarship.

Texas Association for Marriage and Family Therapy   January 1995
Recipient of the TAMFT Student Achievement Award (as a Master's Degree student).

PRACTICA/PREDOCTORAL INTERNSHIP PSYCHOTHERAPY EXPERIENCE

Salvation Medical Center   Sept 1998–Feb 1999
Department of Behavioral Medicine   Supervisor: Peter Neater,
Behavioral Health Section   PhD
Friendliness, Texas
Provided psychological assessment, individual and group therapy to military families
and their dependents; worked as part of an interdisciplinary team throughout various
departments within the medical setting to provide psychological intervention and
consultation with patients, nurses, rehabilitation therapists, and physicians.

The Inman Christian Center   June 1997–Aug 1997
Inner-City Community Center   Supervisors: Chris Lopez,
Friendliness, Texas   PhD
Developed and conducted psychoeducational and social skills groups with children
living in poverty and in violent neighborhoods.

Community Counseling Service   Aug 1994–June 1999
My University   Supervisors: Somé
Friendliness, Texas   Phaculty, PhD
Provided individual, marriage, and family therapy primarily to minority low-income
clients, as well as university students.

Solution Workshop, Counseling Offices   June 1995–Dec 1997
Private Practice   Supervisors: Fred Spread,
Friendliness, Texas   PhD & Maggie
                                               Miller, PsyD
Provided individual, marriage, and family therapy to members of the Police Depart-
ment, Fire Department, and EMS personnel; grief counseling due to family deaths
including on-the-job fatalities; Critical Incident Stress Debriefing.

The Center for Health Care Services   Dec 1994–Dec 1995
Mental Health Services   Supervisor: Tim Notnow,
Friendliness, Texas   MA
Provided in-home therapy to low-income families with a chronically mentally ill
family member.

PROVISION OF PSYCHOTHERAPY SUPERVISION

The University of Psychology   August 1999–Present
University Counseling Center
My City, Illinois
Provided weekly individual supervision to counseling/developmental psychology doc-
toral students providing services at the University Counseling Center.

Grayson Square Health Care Center,   Apr 1997–June 1999
Colonial Park Manor/Heart of Texas,
Regent Care Center (Nursing Homes)
Friendliness, Texas
Supervised graduate practicum students of University providing individual, couples, family, and group therapy with the nursing home residents and their families. The nursing home clients suffer from dementia, as well as chronic psychiatric illnesses, and some clients are recovering substance abusers with resultant organic dysfunction.

Community Counseling Service   Jan 1996–June 1999
My University
Friendliness, Texas
Provided live supervision to closed therapy teams composed of Master's Degree practica students each semester; provided individual supervision and case consultation to Master's students.

PROFESSIONAL PRESENTATIONS

Chameleon, C. (1999, August). Training opportunities in extra-sensory perception. In *Opportunities and challenges for psychologists in the evolving health care marketplace.* American Psychological Association Annual Convention, Boston, MA.

Chameleon, C., with Levant, R. E., & Blatt, A. (1999, August). Expanding roles for psychologists by using ESP: A training paradigm. In *Are We Being Trained for the Jobs of Tomorrow?* Symposium conducted at the American Psychological Association Annual Convention, Boston, MA.

Princess, M., & Chameleon, C. (1999, August). *Student leaders discuss ESP for everyone: A townhall meeting.* American Psychological Association Annual Convention, Boston, MA.

PUBLICATIONS

Chameleon, C. (1998). ESP for everyone. In F. N. Thomas & T. S. Nelson (Eds.), *Tales from family therapy: Life-changing clinical experiences.* New York: Haworth Press.

Chameleon, C. (1997). Understanding ESP. In K. Doka & J. Davidson (Eds.), *Living with your powers: When mental illness is prolonged.* New York: Taylor & Francis.

Personal and Professional References Are Available Upon Request

Sample Curriculum Vitae 2

Henrietta Hypothetical
555 Maple Square
Indianapolis, Indiana 55555
(123) 456-7890
Email Address Here

Education:

PsyD Candidate, Clinical Psychology
Indiana University of Great People, Indianapolis, Indiana
American Psychological Association-approved program
2002 (anticipated completion)

MA, Clinical Psychology, August 1999
Indiana University of Great People, Indianapolis, Indiana

BA, Psychology, May 1996
Harvard University, Boston, Massachusetts

Honors:

Undergraduate Dean's List: Three semesters
Emerson Scholarship
PSI CHI National Psychology Honor Society, September 1994–current
Eastern Collegiate Science Conference/MA State Undergraduate Psychology
 Conference Award, April 1995
Graduate Merit Scholarship, 1997/1998 academic year

Professional Involvement:

Student Affiliate of American Psychological Association, since 1997
Student Member of the National Academy of Neuropsychology, since 1998
Student Member of the American Psychological Society, since 2000
Campus Representative for the Advocacy Coordinating Team of the American
 Psychological Association of Graduate Students (APAGS), since 2000

University Involvement:

Graduate Student Assembly Member, 8/97 to 5/99
Graduate Student Judicial Board Member, 8/99 to current

Presentations:

Hypothetical, H., Out, D. C., & Clearfield, T. V. (1995, April). *The role of positive affect and making movies: Acting our way to a better mood.* Paper presented at the 49th Annual Eastern Colleges Science Conference.

Hypothetical, H., Manhattan, P., Townsend, M., & Piccolo, R. (1999, November). *How to negotiate a more adult-to-adult relationship with your parents.* Lecture Series Presentation.

Hypothetical, H., & Gillespie, M. N. (2000, February). *Interpersonal attraction: Theories of love and relationships in psychology.* A workshop conducted for gifted youth in Indianapolis County, Indianapolis University of Great People, Indianapolis, IN.

Hypothetical, H. (2000, April). *Social support following traumatic brain injury.* Poster presentation at the Spring 2000 meeting of the Indianapolis Psychological Association.

Clinical Experience:

May 2000–present   **Outpatient Therapist**
                        Indianapolis County Guidance Center
                        Indianapolis, Indiana

Provided individual and group psychotherapy to a wide variety of clients, with an emphasis on community members with minimal social and economic resources. Therapeutic issues included major depressive disorder, schizophrenia, head injury, as well as other neurotic and psychotic disorders. Provided services to approximately eight individual clients on a weekly basis, as well as one weekly group session. Participated in weekly staff meetings, in-service trainings, case consultations, and supervision sessions. Interacted with various managed care companies when necessary for reimbursement and continuation of services.

Supervisor: Mel Gibson, PhD

August 1998–May 2000   **Graduate Assistant**
                            Learning Center
                            Indiana University of Great People

Taught series of workshops related to college student mental health issues. Assisted students in coursework. Addressed course-scheduling concerns with students and prepared schedules for following semester. Assisted in research on the effectiveness of vocabulary coursework in college, nontraditional students' experience of college, student attitudes towards classroom behavior, and sexual orientation discrimination among college students.

Supervisor: Sharon Stone, PhD

September 1999–present   **Practicum Student**
                             Alligator General Hospital
                             Indianapolis, Indiana

Administration and scoring of assessment materials, as well as report writing, focusing on neuropsychological assessment. Primary populations served include both inpatient and outpatient assessment of individuals with traumatic brain injury, dementia, psychiatric illness, pre- and post-ECT treatment, and exposure to toxins.

Supervisor: Jennifer Lopez, PhD
Supervised Practicum Hours: 600

January 1999–present	**Practicum Student**
	Eating Disorders Clinic
	Center for Applied Psychology
	Indiana University of Great People

Provided individual psychotherapy to an adult population, focusing on eating disorders. Interventions included behavioral, cognitive, interpersonal, and psychodynamic interventions. Participated in live, team, and individual supervision weekly.

Supervisor: Greg Keilin, PhD
Supervised Practicum Hours: 225

September 1999–August 1999	**Practicum Student**
	Adult Treatment Clinic
	Center for Applied Psychology
	Indiana University of Great People

Provided individual psychotherapy to an adult population, focusing on Axis I and Axis II diagnoses. Interventions included behavioral, cognitive, psychodynamic, and experiential orientations. Participated in live, individual, and team supervision weekly.

Supervisor: Santa Claus, PhD
Supervised Practicum Hours: 460

January 1999–August 1999	**Practicum Student**
	Assessment Clinic
	Center for Applied Psychology
	Indiana University of Great People

Conducted assessments on college students and adult referrals from the community. These included a court custody evaluation, learning disability and psychodiagnostic assessments, neuropsychology assessments, and police academy applicant screenings. Utilized cognitive, achievement, personality, neuropsychological, and behavioral measures. Participated in weekly staff meeting, individual and team supervision.

Supervisor: Carol Williams-Nickelson, PsyD
Supervised Practicum Hours: 750

January 1998–May 1998	**Practicum Student**
	Therapeutic Techniques Lab
	Indiana University of Great People

Participated in weekly training and practice of therapeutic skills. Conducted an intake evaluation and provided individual psychotherapy to one client based on an integrative model. Obtained live weekly individual supervision.

Supervisors: Ben Affleck, PsyD; Matt Damon, PhD
Supervised Practicum Hours: 50

August 1997–May 1998	**Graduate Assistant**
	Clinical Psychology Department
	Indiana University of Great People

Responsible for subject recruitment, data collection, and data coding and entering for research on both color perception and mood inducement in artwork, as well as the role that keeping an emotionally focused journal about traumatic experiences has on physical health. The former study included asking subjects to rate a series of artistic postcards on various dimensions related to mood. The second study consisted of instructing individuals to journal about a personal, traumatic experience and reviewing these entries to assess for the potential need to refer to counseling services. Further responsibilities included supervising undergraduate, honors research.

Supervisor: Adam Sandler, PhD

September 1996–July 1997   **Mental Health Advisor**
H.O.M.E.S., Inc.
Boston, Massachusetts

Assisted consumers with chronic mental illness, predominately schizophrenia, in setting and accomplishing personalized goals. Worked on improving independent living skills. Participated in creating and implementing behavioral management strategies. Provided supportive counseling. Collaborated with various community service agencies to assist consumers in gaining access to social, educational, and recreational opportunities. Other responsibilities included the monitoring, record keeping, and supervision associated with the self-administration of medication, as well as the planning of various recreational and social activities and the filing of various personal and medical documents.

Supervisor: Rosie O'Donnell, MA

September 1995–May 1996   **Teaching Assistant**
Research Design and Statistical Analysis Course
Cognitive Psychology Course
Psychology Department
Harvard, Boston, Massachusetts

Coordinated and coded students' work. Provided structured office hours to assist students in related coursework. Reviewed exams with students and assisted needy students in exam preparation. Tutored students in statistics during biweekly individual sessions and pre-exam group sessions. Filed various documents related to courses. Assisted in preparation of lecture topics based upon student questions and academic needs.

Supervisor: Tipper Gore, PhD

Training Experience:

- First Aid and CPR Certification, October 1996
- Medication Certification, October 1996
- Crisis Intervention Training, November 1996
- Direct Care Staff Training, November 1996
- Effective Communication Training, December 1996
- Group Dynamics Training, March 1997
- Disaster Mental Health Services Training—Red Cross, June 2000

Community Involvement:

Red Cross Volunteer, Indianapolis, Indiana   June 2000–current
Participated in disaster mental health service training.

Humane Society Volunteer, Indianapolis, Indiana   March 1994–December 1995
Meals on Wheels, Boston, Massachusetts
Delivered meals to homebound individuals.

GIAC Afterschool Care Center   February 1993–July 1994
Boston, Massachusetts

Professional Development:

Brief Therapy: Lasting Impressions: A 5-day series of seminars/workshops
    Workshops attended: "The Transtheoretical Approach to Patients, Popula-
        tions, and Organizations" Jimmy Dean, PhD
    "The Personal Growth and Development of the Clinician" Mary Smith, PhD
    "Brief Rational Emotive Behavior Therapy" Ally McBeal, PhD

9th Annual Rotman Research Institute Conference: A 5-day series of seminars
    Traumatic Brain Injury: Diagnosis, Outcome, and Rehabilitation

Research:

April 1995
Hypothetical, H., Williams, C., and Campbell, J. H.
Female Athletes and Eating Disorders: Epidemological Perspectives
Supervisor: Mitchell Prinstein, PhD
Site: Harvard, Boston, Massachusetts

June 1999 to current
Hypothetical, H. (in progress)
Social Support for Alzheimer Family Caregivers
Supervisor: Shane Lopez, PhD
Site: Lopez General Hospital, Indianapolis, Indiana

May 2000 to current
Doctoral Dissertation (in progress)
Title: *Understanding Alzheimer's Disease and Related Dementias*
Dissertation chairperson: Sammy Sosa, PhD
Committee members: Jacklyn Smith, PhD, Greg Keilin, PhD
Dissertation proposal defense: 7/00 expected
Dissertation defense: 4/01 expected

CURRICULUM VITAE

John Jacob J. Schmidt

Office
University of X
1011 X Parkway
East Nowhere, State 99999
(444) 234-5678
(444) 345-6789 (FAX)

Home
2 Myhouse St.
City, State 99999
(444) 123-4567

E-Mail: Johnjacob@school.edu

EDUCATION

PhD Candidate
2007

Psyched USA, Mail-order Correspondence Course
Clinical Psychology
Dissertation Chairperson: Sally Struthers, PhD

Master's of Science
2004

Psyched USA, Mail-order Correspondence Course
Clinical Psychology

Bachelor of Arts
2002

Mall of the Americas, Minneapolis, MN
Major: Psychology

HONORS AND AWARDS

2001

"Lassie Award," National Association of Canine
Counseling

2000

Student Travel Award to the Aura of Venus

PROFESSIONAL AFFILIATIONS

American Association of Sandbox Therapy
Society for Research on Psychic Powers
Coalition of Pet Psychotherapists
National Consortium of Un-licensable Therapists

Clinical Experiences

FORMAL PRACTICA TRAINING

July 2001–present
Psychology Intern

Drive-Thru Outpatient Psychotherapy Clinic
Mall of America Food Court
Conducted short-term diagnostic evaluations of children, adolescents, and adults. Treatments included brief counseling and french fries.
Supervisor: Joe, the Manager at Burger King

| July 2000–October 2001 | **Internet Chat-Room Counseling Service** |
| Psychology Intern | Star Trek Chat Room, America OnInternet |

Conducted reflective listening (i.e., cut and paste) treatment of social phobics with preservative interests in science fiction series. Included extensive experience with group therapy.
Supervisors: William Shatner, PhD; Leonard Nemoy, PhD

ADDITIONAL CLINICAL EXPERIENCES

| July 1999–August 1999 | **Psychic Friends Network** |
| Volunteer | Dionne Warwick Center for Psychic Treatment |

Conducted long-term teletherapy using a telepathic therapeutic approach involving long periods of silence.
Supervisors: Miss Cleo, MA

Research Experience

GRANTS FUNDED

Principal Investigator	**Department of Research Award**
July 2002–July 2004	Melatonin and You: A Treatment-Outcome Study
	($100.00)

PRESENTATIONS AND PUBLICATIONS

Schmidt, J. J. J. (2001, August). *Morris revisited: Narcissistic personality traits in the common household feline.* Paper presented at the Purina Conference on the Study of Feline Behavior.

Schmidt, J. J. J., & Struthers, S. (in press). Observations of shopping behavior in a community mall sample. *Journal of The Gap.*

REFERENCES
My Mom, Mrs. Schmidt. 101 Humble Way, City, State 22222
Her Mom, Grandma Schmidt. mommaschmidt@granny.com

5 THE INTERVIEW

Mitchell J. Prinstein

The submission of your application materials is an accomplishment worthy of celebration and much relief. This milestone also begins a sometimes agonizing waiting period that ends once you receive your first notification decision regarding interviews. Sites vary considerably in the proportion of applicants who are invited for an interview. Although some sites invite all applicants for a visit, most extend invitations to 5 to 10 applicants for every available internship slot. This chapter covers the basic information needed to successfully manage the interview process.

SCHEDULING INTERVIEWS

You can expect to hear from internship sites about interview decisions in late November through early January. Most interviews occur in January. Some sites allow you to choose the date of your visit from many choices, whereas others may have only one or two dates to interview all invited applicants. Scheduling interviews can be a logistical challenge, and it is sometimes necessary and permissible to call an internship site to ask whether you have been invited for an interview there so that you can coordinate difficult travel plans. Many APPIC-member sites are now trying to provide notification of interviews around the same time to help students better plan their travel schedules. Be sure to allow for at least one day to regroup between each interview; the itineraries can be quite exhausting.

Interview Formats

Open house interviews. Some sites welcome all applicants to visit the internship site as part of an "open house." For many sites, attendance at the open house is not mandatory to gain admission and may not increase your chances of being selected. It is sometimes difficult to schedule one-on-one interviews with potential supervisors during the open house meeting, but the meeting could be useful for those who wish to obtain information about a program that could not be conveyed in a brochure or by telephone.

Exhibit 5.1. *Interview Checklist*

_____	Site brochure and materials
_____	Copy of your application and essays
_____	Extra copies of your CV
_____	Research abstracts (for sites that emphasize research training)
_____	Professional attire
_____	Personal items

Telephone interviews. Some sites exclusively conduct telephone interviews; others may offer a telephone interview to applicants who are unable to schedule an in-person interview for whatever reason. Many applicants have successfully matched at sites at which they participated in a telephone rather than in-person interview. This is a reasonable option for those applicants unable to travel to a site, although obviously it is not possible to view the facility without the in-person visit.

Site visits/in-person interviews. The vast majority of interviews occur in-person at the internship site. The structure of the interviews can vary considerably. Although group interviews, including multiple applicants and faculty members, are possible, most interviews will be one-on-one, lasting for 30 to 60 minutes. Some of your interviews will be very structured; you may be asked a series of standardized questions to assess the breadth and depth of your clinical experience. Other interviews may be extremely informal; in fact, interviews may consist of friendly conversation with a supervisor about topics unrelated to psychology. Still other interviews may focus entirely on questions you have about the site, requiring you to maintain the conversation and fill the interview time with many questions.

Your meetings may take place in a faculty member's office, while you are touring the facility, or during a lunch. You may even have the chance to explore the facility on your own.

Some sites will have a full day of interviews scheduled for you, meetings from breakfast through the end of the day. Other sites may schedule only two or three appointments with faculty or interns.

Interview Checklist: Before You Go

You can use the interview checklist (see Exhibit 5.1) to be sure you have all of the necessary materials for the site visit.

- It is a good idea to bring along a copy of the site materials on your site visit to review before beginning the interview day. Interviewers usually prefer to spend the meeting time discussing information that you could not have obtained from their site brochure. A quick review of the site materials will also help remind you of the experiences that made you most interested in the site when you applied.

- A review of your application also is helpful before beginning the interview day. You will undoubtedly be asked to discuss your perceptions regarding the match between your interests and the training site experiences. It is best to review the points you stated in your essay to prepare for answering this question.
- In many cases, you will know more about the training site than each interviewer knows about you. Not all interviewers have had access to your application before meeting you. Bring along a few copies of your curriculum vitae (CV)—you may be asked for them.
- Sites that emphasize research as well as clinical training might offer an opportunity to meet with a potential research supervisor. Much like you did when applying for graduate programs, you may want to review potential supervisors' research abstracts to help you develop informed questions regarding their work. Keep in mind that for most clinical internships, including many research-oriented internship sites, a thorough review of supervisors' research is not necessary.
- Many applicants have questions regarding appropriate attire on the internship interview. The answer is simple: Dress professionally—whatever that means for you. As a benchmark, it may be helpful to know that most male applicants wear a coat and tie on the interview day; occasionally they wear a suit. Female applicants should consider wearing a dress, dress-suit or pant-suit with nylons, business shoes, and small jewelry. Dress as you would if you were on a job interview in the business world. However, it is most important that you are comfortable and genuine. Resist the urge to wear an item of clothing or jewelry that will help you to "stand out" from among the other applicants, and attempt instead to differentiate yourself based on your qualifications, social skills, enthusiasm, and unique match to the site.

THE "BIG 3"   If you have been selected for an interview, you already likely possess the minimal qualifications needed to gain admission to the internship site. The interview process is a sorting process to help sites and applicants determine the extent to which there is a match. There is less focus on your credentials and more on your general demeanor and interests. If you effectively communicate that you are high in social skills, enthusiasm, and match (i.e., the "Big 3"), then you have succeeded on the interview.

Social Skills

This seems obvious, and it is. Do not worry about whether you should accept a cup of coffee if offered, whether you should hold doors open for others, and so forth. Simply be appropriate, professional, and considerate. Use your clinical skills. Some interviews will be conversations about the location, your experiences as a graduate student, or reminiscences about people you both know professionally. Have fun and use humor! And if you get tired, remember, just be a LOSER:

    L – Lean forward
    O – Open posture—do not cross your arms over yourself
    S – Sit straight and squarely
    E – Maintain Eye contact
    R – Relax

Enthusiasm

You will be tired from travel or travel delays. You may have several interviews in just a week and are finding it difficult to remember the most pertinent facts about each site. You may have decided that a different site is your first choice and find it hard to appear interested in anyplace else. This is when it is most important to remember to convey enthusiasm to your hosts.

Internship sites would like to select someone who will be happy to be there, who will smile at work, and who seems energetic about the rotations and other opportunities. During the interview, let them know that you are this person.

Following are some examples to help you convey enthusiasm:

Bad No. 1

Interviewer: Welcome to Internship X. Did you have any trouble getting here?

You: Well, my plane was canceled last night because of the storm, and I actually just flew out here at 6:00 this morning. I'm tired and angry at the airline. I always have problems with X airline. What about you? Do you hate X airline? At any rate, I hope this interview is worth it.

Better No. 1

Interviewer: Welcome to Internship X. Did you have any trouble getting here?

You: I was a little concerned with that storm yesterday, but I am excited to be here on time.

Bad No. 2

Interviewer: We do a lot of work with adults who have chronic schizophrenia. Do you have any experience with this population?

You: Actually, I don't. Will that be negotiable?

Better No. 2

Interviewer: We do a lot of work with adults who have chronic schizophrenia. Do you have any experience with this population?

You: No, I haven't had a chance to do that yet, but I think that would be a great experience for me.

Bad No. 3

Interviewer: This rotation will involve a lot of assessment with children, and I see that you already have a lot of that experience. Is that something you are OK with?

You: Yeah, I guess. I figured I'd have to do more of that on internship, and that's fine if I have to do it.

Better No. 3

Interviewer: This rotation will involve a lot of assessment with children, and I see that you already have a lot of that experience. Is that something you are OK with?

You: I enjoy assessment, and I think that it would be good for me to develop that as a specialty. That sounds like it would be a great opportunity for me at this point in my training.

Match

You must emphasize that you are a unique match to the internship site. It is a big mistake to believe that the match is clear or obvious simply because you have similar training experiences or because others in your graduate program previously were placed at that site. Remember that the faculty members may interview 5 or 10 times as many applicants as they have slots, and it is likely that they may have spent less time with your application than you have spent looking over their site materials. You need to show them the match—explicitly.

Some examples include the following:

Bad No. 1

Interviewer: What can I tell you about the rotation I supervise here at the VA?

You: Well, you tell me. What would an intern's experiences be on your rotation?

Better No. 1

Interviewer: What can I tell you about the rotation I supervise here at the VA?

You: Actually, a primary goal for me is to get experience working in a VA. I think I may want to work in this kind of position one day. So, I am particularly interested in this rotation. What would a typical intern's experience be like here?

Bad No. 2

Interviewer: Hi. You must have been asked a lot of questions already, so why don't I let you ask me something? What do you want to know?

You: OK, um, I dunno know, um, do you like being here in Montana?

Better No. 2

Interviewer: Hi. You must have been asked a lot of questions already, so why don't I let you ask me something? What do you want to know?

You: OK. Well, since I am really interested in getting experience with A, B, and C on internship, I was especially excited to hear about Rotations A, B, and C. They seem to be a perfect match to my interests and skills. I have never lived in Montana, however. What is that like?

Bad No. 3

Interviewer: You come from a behavioral program, but this rotation involves a lot of experience with the Rorschach. Do you think you will fit here?

You: I am a quick learner. I've heard the Rorschach is fairly easy, and I think I will fit just fine here.

Better No. 3

Interviewer: You come from a behavioral program, but this rotation involves a lot of experience with the Rorschach. Do you think you will fit here?

You: Interesting you should mention that—one of my goals for internship was to approach assessment from a broader perspective, so the opportunity to get Rorschach experience would be a great fit for me.

A list of sample questions that you may be asked during interviews is included in Exhibit 5.2. It may be helpful for you to construct written responses to these questions to help crystallize your thoughts. Revisit your answers after a week or two, and determine if they are an accurate and good reflection of you, your experiences, and your interests. Practice these responses aloud; you will be surprised to find that it is initially difficult to articulate your responses smoothly and confidently.

ASK, ASK, AND ASK AGAIN

You will be asked many questions on the interview day, and your responses to them will help the site get to know you a bit better. You will also have a chance to ask questions. In fact, you will likely have more interviews during which you are the inquisitor rather than the respondent, so it is essential that you are prepared with many questions about the site. Lists of sample questions for faculty and interns are included here (see Exhibits 5.3 and 5.4, respectively), but remember that these lists may be used by many applicants—so do not ask these questions verbatim. Use this list to help generate some questions of your own.

The manner in which you ask these questions should capture the same themes as noted earlier and help continue to communicate that you are socially skilled, enthusiastic, and a good match. Examples include the following:

Bad No. 1

You: So, you're the supervisor for the ADHD rotation. Can you tell me about it?

Better No. 1

You: I have been looking forward to meeting you because I am especially excited about the ADHD rotation. Can you tell me what opportunities interns have on this rotation?

Bad No. 2

You: Yes, do people actually enjoy living in Idaho? Is there anything to do for fun around here?

Exhibit 5.2. *Questions You May Be Asked*

1. Tell me about yourself.
   - Break the statement down.
   - Start with professional interests and goals but consider saying, "I'd also be happy to talk about some of my personal interests." (This shows that you are multidimensional, that is, you do have a life outside of psychology.)
2. Why did you apply to our program?
   - Outline goals and training match
   - Rotations
   - Your training experiences
   - Their setting
   - Research, if applicable
   - Any extras or unique opportunities.
3. What do you want to get out of our internship (training goals)?
   - Investment in training (e.g., it fits well; you have studied their brochure, and it feels right)
   - Multidisciplinary setting—excellent training ground
   - You can make contributions (describe), plus learn, gain more experience, obtain guidance, and develop expertise
   - Mentorship and good professional relationships with faculty.
4. What things do you want to work on during internship?
5. What research would you want to pursue here?
6. What is the status of your dissertation?
7. Why did you choose clinical/counseling psychology?
8. What are the strengths of your graduate program?
9. What are the limitations of your graduate program?
10. Why should we select you as an intern? Match with program?
11. Tell me about your
    - Clinical experience
    - Assessment experience
    - Research experience
    - Most difficult client situation and how you handled it.
12. What is your primary theoretical orientation? Why?
13. What would you be doing if you were not in psychology?
14. What are your personal strengths and weaknesses?
15. What are your clinical strengths and weaknesses?
16. What are your professional (collegial) strengths and weaknesses?
17. What population have you found it most difficult to work with?
18. Has any client or patient ever challenged your fundamental beliefs about life? What was that experience like? How did you manage it?
19. What are you looking for in supervision?
20. Who was your favorite supervisor? Why?
21. Who was your least favorite supervisor? Why?
22. Tell me about a negative supervisory experience.
23. Tell me about a rewarding supervisory experience.
24. How do you work with and understand people with different ethnic or cultural backgrounds?
25. Do you have a master's degree? In what?
26. What nonpsychology work experience has helped to shape your professional identity?
27. Why did you select the dissertation topic that you did?
28. Tell me about an ethical problem that you faced and how you handled it.
29. What are your future goals in psychology?
30. Where do you think the profession is heading?
31. What do you think about prescription privileges (or any other hot national psychology topic)?
32. What is your favorite or most influential psychology book?
33. What is your favorite nonpsychology book?
34. What else would you like me to know about you that is not on your CV?
35. What do you do in your spare time?
36. Tell me about your most rewarding case.
37. Tell me about your toughest case.

Exhibit 5.3.   *Questions to Ask Internship Faculty*

1. What is a typical day like for an intern here?
2. What are you looking for in an intern?
3. What has the impact of managed care been on the program (if applicable)? How has it affected the rotation(s)? Affected the length of stay? Affected the role of the intern?
4. Do you anticipate changes in your program in the next year (rotations, staff)?
5. What is the relationship between psychology and psychiatry departments here? Other disciplines? Other offices?
6. What do you think the strengths of this internship are?
7. What do interns usually do after internship?
8. Are there opportunities for post-docs here?
   - Conveys that you are excited about internship and your career; will be applying for post-docs, jobs, and so forth.
   - What kind of professional guidance is offered?
   - Are they supportive through the post-doc and job-seeking process?
   - Does the internship play an active role in trying to place its graduates?
9. Ask if not explained in materials
   - Seminars and educational opportunities or didactics and typical topics?
   - Intern evaluation process? Quality? Frequency? By whom?
   - Do they strive for breadth or specialty training?
10. Treatment opportunities
    - Individual/group/families/couples/age ranges?
    - Specific populations?
    - Typical referral questions on a specific rotation?
    - Proportion of inpatient and outpatient?
    - Continuity of care? Can you follow the patient from an inpatient stay on an outpatient basis?
    - Inpatient severity of pathology? Length of stay? Role of intern on the unit?
    - How are rotations assigned?
    - How are patients assigned to treatments? Flexibility in assignments?
11. Supervision
    - How are supervisors assigned?
    - Individual/group?
    - Hours per week or case?
    - Live? Video? Audio?
    - How many supervisors does each intern have?
    - Theoretical orientation of supervisors? Which is most strongly represented?
12. Assessment
    - Center's assessment philosophy?
    - Availability?
    - Typical frequency?
    - Emphasis?
    - Neuropsych?
    - Opportunities outside of rotations?
    - Projectives?
    - Proportion of assessment to therapy?
13. Research
    - How strong of an emphasis do you place on research?
    - What are the opportunities for research?
    - How are research topics selected?
    - What activities might you have the opportunity to become involved with?
    - "I understand you are conducting research in X. Would an incoming intern have the opportunity to work with you in that area?"
14. Resources
    - Computer support?
    - Office?
    - Treatment rooms?
    - Referral agencies?
15. Is there ever a need to travel to other satellite clinics?
16. Are interns ever on call after hours?
17. How are emergencies managed? What is the typical frequency of emergencies?

Exhibit 5.4. *Questions to Ask the Current Interns*

1. Example of a workday/week: Typical activities? Hours per day/week? Meetings? Didactics?
   - Amount of work you take home?
   - What types of assessments?
   - How much time on assessment?
   - How many assessments per week? Write them at work or at home?
2. How is time divided among assessment, treatment, consultation, and psychotherapy?
3. Role of interns at site? With faculty?
4. Relationship between interns and faculty?
   - Do you feel that you are highly regarded by the faculty?
   - Supervision satisfaction?
   - Availability? On site if you encounter a problem?
5. Strengths of the program? Best thing?
6. Limitations/disappointments with the program? Worst thing?
7. Physical resources: Computer? Office space? Treatment rooms? Phone? Beeper?
8. On-call hours?
9. Paperwork?
10. Health care:
    - Quality?
    - Satisfactory?
11. Time to work on dissertation?
12. Rotations
    - What rotations are you doing?
    - Most rewarding?
    - Least rewarding?
    - Support among the interns?
    - Number of interns on rotations at a time (one or more than one)?
    - Hours?
    - Supervision?
13. Cost of living?
14. Availability of affordable housing?
15. Do you like the city?
16. Do you socialize with faculty? With other interns?
17. Time for fun?
18. What has your experience at the site been like?
19. What has helped and impeded your adjustment to the site?
20. Where are you from? What program? What type of program?
21. What influenced your decision to select this internship?
22. For you, a year ago, what didn't you ask that would be important to know?

Better No. 2

You: Living in Idaho would be a new experience for me. Can you tell me what you have enjoyed about this location?

Bad No. 3

You: Do most people get jobs in private practice when they leave this internship?

Better No. 3

You: I am really looking forward to beginning my private practice after internship, and I hear that this site offers good training experiences to help with that. Has that been the experience of most prior interns?

Bad No. 4

You: I hear that there is not much data out there supporting the incremental validity of measures like the Rorschach beyond what one could learn from a good diagnostic interview. How come ya'll still administer that measure?

Better No. 4

You: I come from a program that does not emphasize training in projective assessments, but I notice that is a large component of the rotation that you supervise. What is your position on the recent debates regarding evidence-based assessment and treatment?

THANK YOU
NOTES

Thank you notes are not necessary, and the presence or absence of a note or particular type of note (e.g., e-mail, typed letter) will not influence the decision of the admission committee. However, thank you notes are a courteous, appropriate way to express gratitude to your hosts, and therefore, the practice is quite common among intern applicants.

In addition to an expression of gratitude, thank you notes offer a final opportunity to express your interest in the site and explicitly state your perception of a match between the site and your interests. Again, the format of the note—whether e-mail or letter, handwritten or typed—is not at all important. Let the note be an extension of your own style and the level of professionalism that you have communicated throughout the application process. Several sample thank you notes have been included at the end of this chapter as examples.

Applicants often face a dilemma when deciding whether to send separate thank you notes to each person with whom they interviewed at one site or to send a note only to the training director. Again, there is no wrong answer. E-mail notes can be easily forwarded to many, but individually typed letters to more than a dozen faculty at a site may be a bit excessive.

A few suggestions when writing thank you notes include the following:

- Thank you notes may demonstrate initiative and genuine interest, and they can set you apart from other applicants. Keep them simple, and make them personal if you are able.
- Follow-up can be another opportunity to highlight something positive about your CV, experience, training, or interview. Send your note within 1–2 days after your interview so they will remember you when they receive the note.

Sample Thank You Note 1

January 24, 2003

Dear Dr. X,

I enjoyed meeting with you on January 16, and I am very impressed with your program. Speaking with you, Dr. X, Dr. X, and the current interns was helpful to me in forming a more complete understanding of the XXX Consortium.

Overall, I believe that the rotations and experiences offered at XXX match my goals for internship training. Additionally, the pediatric research opportunities are another attractive aspect of your training program.

In addition to the variety of training opportunities, I was greatly impressed by the friendliness and warmth of the people at XXX. I believe that I would be happy and honored to work with everyone with whom I met during my visit.

I am very enthusiastic about my visit to XXX. As per our conversation on January 23, I believe that XXX provides an optimal fit with my previous experiences and future interests for internship training.

Sincerely,

Your Name

February 1, 2003

Dear Dr. X,

I wanted to thank you for taking the time to meet with me to discuss my internship application and your program. After hearing so many positive things about the internship from friends and colleagues, it was nice to leave the interview day with the same positive feelings myself!

I am very impressed with and excited about the training opportunities your internship has to offer. I feel that your internship's strong adherence to the scientist–practitioner model, with attention devoted to both clinical and research training, is unique among the internship programs I have explored. XXX seems like an ideal place for me to gain breadth in my clinical training, as well as have the opportunity to apply my research skills to areas in pediatric psychology other than pain. Some of the research projects we discussed (e.g. familial transmission in pediatric obesity) were incredibly interesting and exciting to me!

Again, thank you for your time, and I hope that you will consider me for your fine internship.

Sincerely,

Your Name

Sample Thank You Note 3

January 20, 2002

Dear Dr. X,

Thank you for taking the time to meet with me to discuss my internship application and your program. I enjoyed the tour of the hospital and also appreciated hearing about your work; the training opportunities available in the sleep disorders clinic sounded particularly interesting! I am very impressed with your internship program and think that XXX would be an ideal place for me to continue my clinical and research training.

Again, thank you for your time, and I hope that you will continue to consider me for your internship.

Sincerely,

Your Name

January 30, 2003

Dear Dr. X and Dr. X,

I appreciated the opportunity to interview with you over the telephone. I was especially struck by the important questions you asked about clinical competency in diversity issues that were embedded in the vignettes posed. Since the telephone interview, I have continued to think about your site, the vignettes, and your brochure. The more I think about the training opportunities at your site, the more excited I become with the thought of being matched to XXX.

I hope to have the opportunity to meet you in person—hopefully by being matched to your site.

Thank you for the invitation to call or write with further questions regarding your internship site. As I learn more about your training philosophy and internship site, I become more and more convinced that XXX would be an ideal match for me.

Sincerely,

Your Name

6 THE MATCH

W. Gregory Keilin

Once the internship interviews have been completed, the next step is to begin thinking about how to navigate the computer Match. The Match was implemented by the Association of Psychology Postdoctoral and Internship Centers (APPIC) in 1999 to deal with an internship selection process that, frankly, had become a nightmare for applicants. Before then, applicants had to deal with pressure tactics, "game-playing," and indirect or inappropriate communication by internship sites. Although the Match has not made internship selection stress-free, it has made a huge difference in the lives of internship applicants.

The Match may seem somewhat daunting at first; however, you will find it to be an easy, straightforward, and user-friendly process. This chapter provides an overview of the process, along with tips about how to make the Match work best for you.

TIMELINE

Your participation in the APPIC Match occurs at three distinct times during the internship selection process:

Date	Activity
September–October	Submit Match registration
Late January–Early February	Construct and submit rank order list (ROL)
Late February	Receive Match results

Each of these activities is described in detail in this chapter.

REGISTRATION

The APPIC Match is conducted by National Matching Services, Inc. (NMS), a company located in Toronto, Canada, specializing in professional matching services. To register for the Match, simply download the registration forms from the NMS Web site, http://www.natmatch.com/psychint. After printing and filling out the forms, mail them to NMS, along with the appropriate fee. An e-mail confirmation of your registration will be sent; it includes your five-digit applicant code number that uniquely identifies you for the purposes of the Match.

You generally should register for the Match in September or early October, as this allows you to receive your applicant code number in time to include it on your internship applications. Remember, though, that the fee is nonrefundable; if you are unsure about whether you will be applying for internship this year, you might want to wait until later in the process to register (but no later than the December 1st registration deadline). If you don't have your applicant code number before you submit your internship applications, don't worry—there will be plenty of time to provide it to internship sites at a later date.

To have your registration properly processed, it is important that you describe your program accurately on your registration form. Applicants who are enrolled in doctoral programs that are APPIC "subscribers" (i.e., a doctoral program gains subscriber status if it pays an annual fee to APPIC for special services and discounts for their students) receive a discount on their Match registration fee. The NMS Web site lists those programs that are subscribers; you also can check with your director of clinical training (DCT) to be certain. APPIC subscriber status is by doctoral program, not by department, school, or university; thus, one doctoral program at your university may be a subscriber while another may not be.

> **TIP:** If your doctoral program is not an APPIC subscriber, consider encouraging them to become one. This reduces the costs for you and other applicants from your doctoral program.

For example, let's say you attend Beachcomber University in Miami, Florida, and the NMS Web site shows the following listing for your university:

Miami	**BEACHCOMBER UNIVERSITY**	**School Code: 999**
	Clinical: Frank A. Johnson, PhD	Subscriber 001
	School: John H. Smith, PsyD	Subscriber 002

In this example, the clinical and school psychology students at Beachcomber University are entitled to the reduced Match fee because both of those programs are listed as APPIC subscribers. However, students enrolled in the counseling psychology program are not entitled to the discount because their program is not listed as an APPIC subscriber.

Once you have completed your Match registration, you won't need to think much more about it until you have completed the application and interview process.

Constructing Your ROL

After the whirlwind of interviewing in January comes to a close and you have had a chance to evaluate each of your internship programs, you will need to determine your order of preference for these programs. Ultimately, you will need to develop a ROL for the Match, which is a list of internship programs in the order in which you prefer them. One important consideration that we cannot overemphasize is:

> **TIP:** The order in which you rank internship programs should reflect only your *true* preferences, without regard for how you think these programs have ranked

you, whether the programs will be ranking you, or what sort of pressure you might have experienced from others to rank programs.

Thus, the program that you are most excited about should be ranked first on your ROL, your next most preferred program should be ranked second, and so forth. Why is this such an important issue? The Match algorithm has been specifically designed to allow you to think only about your own needs and preferences, providing an opportunity for you to make ranking decisions in as pressure-free an environment as possible. The computer has been programmed to respect your rankings, and you will be matched to the highest ranked program on your list that ranks you and doesn't fill its positions with more-preferred applicants. If you deviate from using your true preferences—for example, by trying to guess how a site has ranked you and adjusting your rankings based on this assumption—you will likely end up being matched to a less-preferred program. You will receive the best outcome only if you rank programs in the order in which you want them.

Some additional points to remember about constructing your ROL:

- You may rank as many programs as you wish.
- Your rankings remain confidential. Internship programs will never be told where you have ranked them, either before or after the Match.
- You should generally rank all of the programs at which you are being considered. However, you should omit any program from your list that you consider unacceptable. In other words, if you do not want to be matched to a particular program even if it was the only position available to you in the Match, simply omit that program from your ROL. You cannot be matched to any program that isn't listed on your ROL.
- Each program in the Match has a 4-digit program code number that must be used when constructing your rankings. A list of participating programs and their program code numbers is available on the NMS Web site.
- Some internship sites may have more than one program code number, usually to represent different rotations or training experiences. For example, a site with a neuropsychology rotation and a geropsychology rotation may use a different program code number for each, allowing you to rank the programs separately on your ROL. In addition, sites should clarify for you how their program code numbers are affiliated with which programs, rotations, or training experiences.

To better illustrate the ranking process, let's say that you have applied to several internship programs, and your true preferences for these programs dictate that you rank them in the following order:

Your True Preferences
1. 9989—Really Fine Community Mental Health Center
2. 0008—Better Health Hospital: Neuropsychology Program
3. 9679—Truly Wonderful Medical Center
4. 0009—Better Health Hospital: Geropsychology Program
5. 8229—Sunshine Children's Hospital.

In this illustration, the Better Health Hospital has two separate programs in the Match, each with its own unique program code number. Because you prefer the neuropsychology program over the geropsychology program, these rankings reflect this preference. Let's throw some twists into this scenario with a couple of examples.

Example 1. Let's say that the Sunshine Children's Hospital calls you and tells you that you are a truly wonderful applicant; in fact, they violate Match policies and tell you that they are ranking you as their number 1 choice.

> *Question:* Given this situation, should you move Sunshine higher on your ROL so you don't "miss out" on them?

> *Answer:* Absolutely not. Because your true preference is for Sunshine to be ranked fifth, the best and only approach is to leave them ranked fifth.

If Sunshine Hospital does rank you as their number 1 choice, you will definitely be matched to them only if the computer is unable to match you to the four higher ranked programs on your list. In other words, you haven't reduced your chances of getting matched to Sunshine Children's Hospital by ranking your more-preferred sites higher on your list.

Example 2. Let's say that the Really Fine Community Mental Health Center (CMHC) doesn't seem that interested in you. In fact, even though you got a highly favorable impression of the program during your interview, you suspect that you did a horrible job in responding to their questions. Even with this interview fiasco, they remain your most preferred site.

> *Question:* Given this situation, should you move Really Fine CMHC lower on your list based on your assumption that they aren't going to rank you very highly?

> *Answer:* Absolutely not; you should definitely rank Really Fine CMHC as number 1 on your list.

If the computer is not successful in matching you to Really Fine CMHC, it will simply go to the next site on your list without having penalized you in any way. In other words, by ranking the Really Fine CMHC as number 1, you have not reduced your chances of being matched to any other site on your list. Thus, you don't get penalized for ranking sites that you consider "long-shots."

SUBMITTING YOUR ROL

Once you have constructed your ROL, you then must log in to the NMS Web site to submit your rankings to the Matching program: http://www.natmatch.com/psychint. Click on "Rank Order Lists—Applicants," and use the "Rank Order List Input and Confirmation" (ROLIC) system to enter your rankings. To log in to the ROLIC system, use your applicant code number and the password/PIN that was sent to you by NMS. Entering your rankings via the ROLIC system is a very simple and straightforward process, and complete instructions are available on the NMS Web site. Once you have finished entering your ROL, you must certify it, which designates your list as being complete and ready to use in the Match.

If you change your mind about your rankings before the submission deadline, you can log in again to the ROLIC system and make the appropriate changes to your ROL. You can do this even if your list was previously certified (but be sure to recertify the list once you have made your changes). No changes are permitted once the ROL submission deadline has passed.

> **TIP:** Don't wait until the last day to enter your rankings! You don't want to risk being unable to access the NMS Web site if you encounter Internet connection problems or a busy server.

RECEIVING YOUR RESULTS

Once you have submitted your ROL, there is nothing left to do but wait for the Match processing to take place. There is about a 2 ½-week wait between the ROL submission deadline and the release of the Match results. Although this wait can be excruciating for applicants, this time period is absolutely necessary for NMS to ensure that the Match is conducted accurately. During this period, NMS extensively checks and re-checks the Match processing to ensure that all applicants and programs receive the best possible Match.

The release of the Match results occurs in two steps—generally at 10:00 a.m. EST on a Friday and at the same time the following Monday in late February:

- *Friday:* On this day you will learn whether you have been successfully matched to an internship program, but you will *not* learn the name of that program to which you have been matched. Internship programs are not provided any information on this day.
- *Monday ("APPIC Match Day"):* On this day you will be told the name of the internship program to which you have been matched. Internship programs are also told the names of the applicants to which they have been matched. For those applicants who did not receive any match, the APPIC Clearinghouse begins operating on this day.

Although this two-step release of results may seem like APPIC is trying to torture applicants, there is actually a very good reason for it. Several years ago, APPIC learned that releasing the complete results on one day was extremely difficult for applicants who did not get matched to any internship program, because they had to deal with that very unfortunate news while at the same time having to immediately begin navigating the Clearinghouse. The two-step process just described provides unmatched applicants with a 72-hour period to deal with their feelings about not being matched; to consult with family, friends, and faculty; and to prepare for the opening of the Clearinghouse on Monday morning.

There are three ways for you to obtain your Match results:

- *Via e-mail:* NMS will attempt to send you an e-mail message on both Friday and Monday mornings no later than 10:00 a.m. EST. Keep in mind that e-mail is subject to delays or errors and is thus not 100% reliable (in fact, I estimate that 5%–10% of applicants do not receive this e-mail in a timely fashion). If you don't receive this e-mail, you may use one of the two additional methods described next to obtain your Match results.

- *Via the Internet:* Beginning at 10:00 a.m. EST on Friday and Monday, you may use your applicant code number and password/PIN to log in to the NMS Web site to obtain your results.
- *Via your DCT:* If you are enrolled in an APPIC subscriber doctoral program, your DCT will have access to your Match results.

TIP: NMS actually begins sending result information a couple of hours before the official 10:00 a.m. EST release time. Thus, your results may actually arrive by e-mail early on Friday and Monday morning!

Once you have received the name of the site to which you have been matched on Monday morning, there is one additional detail to take care of—talk to your new training director! Most training directors like to talk to their new interns on this day to provide a personal welcome. Training directors and applicants are allowed to contact each other after 11:00 a.m. EST on Monday (remember that you provided a telephone number on the AAPI where you can be reached between 11:00 a.m. and 1:00 p.m. EST on that morning). If you don't receive a call from your new training director during that period, it is possible that he or she is having difficulty reaching you, and you should call him or her to acknowledge the Match result.

Finally, training directors are required to send you a written appointment agreement, postmarked no later than 72 hours after Match day.

OTHER ITEMS TO KNOW

APPIC Match Policies

APPIC has developed a set of policies that guide the operation of the Match. These policies are available for viewing or downloading on both the APPIC and NMS Web sites and are included with the registration forms that you downloaded. It is imperative that you carefully read these policies before your interviews, as you are expected to abide by them throughout the selection process. APPIC does take action against internship programs and applicants who violate the policies.

Although not a substitute for actually reading the Match policies, here are some of the more important considerations for internship applicants:

1. Applicants and programs are not permitted to communicate, solicit, accept, or use any ranking-related information before the release of the Match results. Furthermore, applicants and programs may never ask about how they have been ranked, even after the release of the Match results. Some examples of what applicants should *never* say to an internship program include:
   - "You are my first choice."
   - "You are one of my top-ranked sites."
   - "I really like your site better than the other sites at which I've interviewed."
   - "Where do you intend to rank me?"
   Even with these restrictions, it is important to understand that the policies are not intended to restrict the expression of genuine interest or enthusiasm about a program. So, here are some examples of what *is* permissible:

- "I have really enjoyed my interview with you today."
- "I am very impressed with your internship program."
- "I really like this neuropsychology rotation, and I really believe that it will meet my training needs."
- "Your internship faculty seem to be very invested in the training needs of your interns."
- "After visiting your inpatient program, I don't think it is quite what I'm looking for. However, I would still very much like to be considered for your outpatient program, as that seems to be a much better fit for me."

So, the best approach is to simply follow the normal guidelines of courteous and professional communication while not making any statements about rankings or about comparing one internship program to another.

2. Each internship program that conducts onsite or telephone interviews must notify you as to whether you will be interviewed no later than the interview notification date listed for that program in the APPIC directory.

3. The results of the Match are binding. Once you submit a ROL to the Match program, you are obligated to attend the internship program to which you are matched. Similarly, the program to which you are matched is required to accept you as an intern for the coming year.

4. After the Match is completed, training directors are required to send you a written appointment agreement outlining the conditions of the appointment, such as stipend, fringe benefits, and the beginning and ending dates of the internship year.

Couples

The APPIC Match has special procedures to assist applicants who are members of a couple when both partners are applying for psychology internships in the same year. These procedures allow a couple to maximize their chances of being located in the same geographic area. Although couples are not required to use these procedures, virtually all couples find it advantageous to do so. More information about this option is available at both the APPIC and NMS Web sites.

Resolving Problems

APPIC has developed two programs to assist applicants who are experiencing difficulties with the selection process or their internship experience:

- *Informal Problem Resolution:* This process allows you to consult confidentially with an APPIC representative to discuss your concerns and to identify options and solutions. If desired, APPIC may become directly involved in negotiating a resolution among parties. Over the past few years, APPIC has found this process to be a highly effective way of resolving difficulties experienced by applicants.
- *Formal Complaints:* APPIC also has a formal complaint process and has established the Standards and Review Committee to handle such complaints. In response to a formal complaint, the APPIC board may impose sanctions on programs or applicants who violate APPIC policies.

APPIC Clearinghouse

The vast majority of internship applicants are successfully placed each year and thus have no need for the APPIC Clearinghouse. However, for those applicants who do need it, the Clearinghouse is an extremely valuable resource about unfilled positions that are available after the Match. The APPIC Web site has extensive information on the operation of the Clearinghouse, including tips and suggestions that have been provided by applicants who have had to navigate the Clearinghouse in previous years.

Staying Informed

Several resources are available that provide additional information about the Match, answer your questions, and generally keep you informed about the process:

- Extensive information is available at the APPIC and NMS Web sites: http://www.natmatch.com/psychint and http://www.appic.org.
- APPIC maintains an e-mail list, MATCH-NEWS, that provides information about the Match directly from the Match coordinator and the APPIC Board of Directors. It is strongly recommended that all applicants subscribe to this list as early as possible in the process. To subscribe, simply send a blank e-mail message to subscribe-match-news@lyris.appic.org. You should receive a confirmation message by return e-mail. This is a low-volume list, generally generating no more than five messages per month. More information on APPIC's e-mail lists can be found at http://www.appic.org; click on "E-mail Lists."
- APPIC also maintains an e-mail discussion, INTERN-NETWORK, that allows current and former intern applicants, training directors, and APPIC board members to discuss various aspects of the selection process. This is a very popular place for internship applicants to get answers to their questions about the AAPI, interviews, the Match, or any other aspect of the process. To subscribe, simply send a blank e-mail message to subscribe-intern-network@lyris.appic.org. This list can generate a lot of e-mail in busy times. Set your subscription to "Digest" mode, which allows you to receive a maximum of one e-mail per day that contains all of the messages that were posted to the list in the preceding 24 hours. To sign up for Digest mode, first subscribe as already described, and then send a blank e-mail to digest-intern-network@lyris.appic.org.
- The APPIC match coordinator, Dr. Greg Keilin, is always happy to answer your questions or assist you with the process. He may be contacted at gkeilin@mail.utexas.edu or (512) 475-6949.

7 FREQUENTLY ASKED QUESTIONS FROM PROSPECTIVE INTERNS

W. Gregory Keilin and Shane J. Lopez

This workbook was originally written as a resource to accompany an internship workshop conducted yearly at the American Psychological Association (APA) convention. At each workshop, prospective interns asked excellent questions about each aspect of the internship application and selection process. The questions posed and addressed in this chapter are representative of those asked at past workshops and of queries submitted to Association of Psychology Postdoctoral and Internship Centers (APPIC) and American Psychological Association of Graduate Students (APAGS) representatives during the application and selection period.

These questions are distributed across the various sections addressing the specific application tasks. The answers are composite responses that the authors of this chapter and the editors of this workbook consider "good advice." Like any advice, you should consider these comments along with your own good judgment and the feedback you have received from your director of clinical training (DCT).

GETTING STARTED *Question 1. How important is it for me to attend an APA-accredited internship program?*

When considering internship programs, students need to be aware of the requirements of three entities: (a) their doctoral program, (b) future licensing boards, and (c) future employers.

- *Regarding your doctoral program:* Some doctoral programs may require an accredited internship to meet graduation requirements. It is important to check with your DCT to be sure that you understand what your program requires.
- *Regarding licensing:* Although many students each year complete nonaccredited internships and experience few, if any, difficulties when applying for licensure, you should be aware of the potential risks associated with nonaccredited internships. A few states may require an APA-accredited internship to qualify

for licensure. Some licensing boards may require additional documentation, or in some cases, additional coursework, for applicants without an accredited internship. For example, at the time of this writing, the State of Texas requires either an APA-accredited internship or an internship that meets a list of specific requirements. Thus, someone attempting to get licensed in Texas who attended a non-APA-accredited internship must demonstrate that their internship meets those requirements. This issue can get especially tricky if you do not know the specific state in which you intend to practice and thus cannot anticipate the future requirements that you will need to meet. For more information, check the requirements of several licensing boards (www.asppb.org) when making your decision.

- *Regarding future employers:* Some employers, such as Veterans Administration (VA) facilities, require an APA-accredited internship for employment. At the VA, this requirement is non-negotiable. Other employers may not have such a strict requirement, although some job and post-doc announcements will specify that an APA-accredited internship is a preferred qualification. Again, because it is difficult to know what your future career plans may be, it is advisable to check with your DCT and as many potential employers as possible to make an educated decision.

Question 2. Is it possible to create my own internship site (e.g., by approaching an agency and asking them to hire me for a year as an "intern")?

Yes, it is possible, but as discussed earlier, it is something that can carry substantial risks for the student in terms of future licensing and employment opportunities. It is also something that many, if not most, doctoral programs would not permit. We generally do not recommend this approach unless you are certain that it will be acceptable to your doctoral program, licensing board, and future employers.

Question 3. What are some ways for me to learn about the selection process and the APPIC Match?

We recommend that students begin learning about the selection process and APPIC Match as early in the process as possible. In particular, students should review the information located at two Web sites: APPIC, http://www.appic.org, and National Matching Services (NMS), http://www.natmatch.com/psychint.

In addition, all applicants should subscribe to the APPIC e-mail list MATCH-NEWS that provides news and information about the Match. A second APPIC e-mail list, INTERN-NETWORK, is a discussion list on which current and former intern applicants, some internship training directors, and APPIC board members discuss various aspects of the selection process.

Question 4. I have some fairly specialized interests and am looking for an internship that will meet these needs. How do I find such an internship?

First, check the APPIC directory to see if the existing search options will allow you to locate an internship that meets your needs. If not, consider submitting an inquiry to the INTERN-NETWORK e-mail list to see if anyone can point you in the right direction. You also might try locating psychologists who are practicing in your area of interest (e.g., through professional organizations, e-mail lists) to see if they have any ideas about internship programs that specialize in this area.

THE AAPI

Question 5. I carefully recorded my clinical hours over the past several years, but now I realize that I neglected to document the specifics about one of my brief training experiences. How do I go about "estimating" my hours?

Documentation of clinical experience typically requires students to report two kinds of information: (a) data about the actual hours spent in professional practice activities and (b) data on the personal characteristics of the clients served in those professional activities. Estimating the data about contact hours may be a simple process if you have a good idea of the number of clients you saw each week. From that bit of data you can extrapolate and generate a good estimate of contact hours over the course of a training experience. Because professionals develop "habits of practice," a proportion of indirect clinical contact to direct contact more than likely is consistent across training experiences. Hence, if you completed 3 hours of indirect service for every 1 hour of direct service in other experiences, chances are good that you engaged in the same kind of clinical balance in this brief training experience.

Estimating the personal characteristics of clientele is more challenging. Referencing the general client data from your training site may be of help. Many sites collect aggregate service data for each month of each year; these data may help remind you about clients you served during that training period. Although it is possible to estimate these important bits of data, no amount of post-experience research or guessing will replace good record-keeping during your training.

Most important, because your DCT is required to sign off on your practicum hours, it is important to discuss with him or her your methods of calculating your hours to ensure that they meet with the DCT's approval.

Question 6. I've had some unique experiences and am confused about how to document them on the AAPI. How do I determine where on the AAPI they should be placed? Similarly, can I include my relevant work experience during my graduate program in my practicum hours?

The first step is to carefully read the instructions that are included with the AAPI, as this is where APPIC has addressed many of the most frequently asked questions about the application.

In general, keep the following points in mind when attempting to document your hours:

- If an experience appears to fall in more than one AAPI category, or doesn't quite fit into any AAPI category, just use your best judgment to select the category that best captures the experience. Do not obsess or worry about it; there is often not a "right" way to classify certain experiences on the AAPI, so just use your judgment about how to document those hours.
- When the exact number of practicum hours or clients seen is not available, your best estimate of these hours is acceptable.
- If you are unsure about how to classify a particular aspect of your experience, consult with your DCT. In addition to being a good resource to answer this type

of question, your DCT must ultimately approve of how you have documented your experience on the AAPI.

- You may only include relevant work experience obtained during your graduate program as part of your practicum hours if your program considers this experience "program sanctioned."
- You may also contact APPIC if you have any questions about completing the AAPI. Contact information is provided in the AAPI instructions.

GOALS AND ESSAYS

Question 7. How personal do I get in the autobiographical essay?

This question is very difficult to answer because every person has a different definition of "personal" information. Some essay readers may like to see some details about a prospective intern's personal (e.g., childhood) experiences and others may find this information irrelevant. Maybe the best answer here is embedded in the preponderance of the comments that internship faculty make about this essay. That is, when internship faculty comment on pitfalls in autobiographical essays, they usually focus on those that are "too personal" rather than those that were not revealing enough. "Too personal" usually relates to discussion of numerous difficult life experiences that have shaped a student's life or to the disclosure of a great deal of personal information that does not necessarily relate to a prospective intern's professional development. On the other hand, some sites argue that students' essays are often not personal enough. Given this anecdotal information, it may be wise to present a balanced view of your personal experiences and to link those experiences directly to your professional development.

Question 8. I am sacrificing some of my goals so that I can complete internship in my immediate geographic region. How do I write my essays to communicate "fit" and be authentic at the same time?

This question suggests that personal values and goals are interfacing with professional values and goals. We believe that striving for that kind of balance is a good approach to the application and selection process. Achieving that balance may be difficult in a selection system that is characterized by "matching" training goals with opportunities. Our belief, however, is that most internship sites offer diverse, quality training experiences that will benefit students and promote their development. Thus, we contend that each internship has something good to offer, and just because it is close to home, its quality should not be discounted. By identifying your goals and values and objectively linking those to the opportunities afforded, you may realize that the "site next door" actually is a good match, as it will promote your development. Hence, you can remain local and be "authentic" about fit. Although we know that this answer is fairly simplistic, as it does not address the many subtle issues embedded in this question, we do believe that some criteria of fit can be met by most quality training sites.

SUPPLEMENTARY MATERIALS

Question 9. I have seen numerous curricula vitae (CVs) that include personal information such as age, marital status, number of children, citizenship, place of birth, and so forth. Any insights about whether selection committees expect or want this information on applicants' CVs would be appreciated.

Our recommendation is to not include such information unless you believe that it is communicating something important about yourself. Having that information on a CV is definitely not an expectation by selection committees.

Question 10. How many letters of recommendation are considered enough but not excessive? Can references be sent to me and I, in turn, forward them to the sites I'm applying to?

There is no clear agreement about this. Many people think you should send only the number of letters requested, whereas others believe that sending one additional letter is a good idea. Under no circumstances should you send more than one additional letter, as this is more likely to annoy selection committees than be helpful to your application.

The advantages to sending an extra letter is that you are protected if one gets lost (or if one of your recommenders doesn't meet the deadline), and it can provide an extra perspective on your competence, which can be helpful to the site. On the other hand, selection committees have a lot of material to read already; in fact, some sites will not read an additional letter if it is included. In addition, having an extra letter requires one other person to take the time to write a letter for you.

Remember that, when it comes to letters of recommendation, more is not necessarily better. For example, having three stellar letters is far better than submitting three stellar letters plus one "good" or "average" letter. So, the bottom line is that there is no right answer to this question. Consider sending either just the number of letters requested or, at most, one more.

Different sites have different requirements about how they want the recommendation letters to arrive (either with the AAPI or directly from the person writing the letter). If a site does not specify a method, then you may decide for that site's application.

THE INTERVIEW

Question 11. Group interviews seem to bring out my competitive spirit. How do I go about "competing" without appearing overly competitive and defensive?

Interviews provide internship faculty with lots of information about applicants' interpersonal skills and coping resources. "Competitiveness" typically is not what faculty is looking for because they may infer that this competitive spirit will cause problems with other interns over the course of a training year. Hence, we encourage you to go into these interview situations with "getting along" rather than "winning the slot" as your number 1 goal; if you get along with people, you have a better chance of winning the slot.

Question 12. Will I have to interpret a Rorschach on my interviews?

We do not have hard data on this issue, but anecdotal information suggests that very few sites and internship faculty require students to demonstrate specific skills during interviews. That is, rarely will you be handed a Rorschach protocol or an SPSS printout and be told to "interpret this." However, you may be asked to present an example of a client who you have worked with, conceptualize cases based on a handful of "facts," or be presented a clinical scenario that requires you to comment on how you would use your multicultural competence to address client needs. Be sure to practice a brief case presentation before you leave for your interviews.

Question 13. What is the best way to deal with APPIC's limitations on the communication of ranking information? How can I still express genuine interest in a program without violating the APPIC Match policies?

The APPIC Match policies prohibit the communication, solicitation, acceptance, or use of ranking-related information. Specifically, this means that it's not OK for you to ask a program how they have ranked you or to tell them how they are ranked with you. Thus, you *cannot* say things like, "Your program is one of my top three choices" or "You are my number one choice."

On the other hand, it is perfectly normal and acceptable for you to communicate your genuine interest, enthusiasm, and excitement about a program without violating these policies. As long as you follow the normal rules of professional and courteous communication, without mentioning rankings, you should be fine. Thus, it is perfectly acceptable to say things like, "I think that this rotation is a great fit for what I am looking for," "I am really excited about the research that you are conducting"; "I have really enjoyed the interview today"; or "This is a terrific program, and I am really impressed with your commitment to training interns."

Question 14. What can I expect to happen after the interview? Will sites stay in contact with me?

Again, contact varies significantly depending on the internship program. Some sites will have no further contact with you after the interview process is over, while others may contact you if they have additional questions or to give you an opportunity to ask questions of them. You really should not try to infer much about a site's interest in you based on how much post-interview contact they do or do not initiate—it really depends on their own approach to the process.

Question 15. What if I have questions for a site—maybe about their program, or whether they have received my application? Is it OK to contact them? If so, what is the best way to do so?

Many students hesitate to contact sites to ask questions about the program, to inquire about application procedures or timelines, and so forth for fear of "bothering" the training director and negatively affecting their application. However, we encourage you to contact a site directly whenever you have questions. The APPIC directory lists the ways in which a site prefers to be contacted (e.g., telephone, e-mail). Most training directors are eager to have you know as much about their program as possible— remember, they are trying to put their best face forward also.

In addition, one of the best ways to find out about a site is to talk with the current interns directly. Interns are often more likely to give you a balanced perspective about the internship experience at the site, including strengths and weaknesses of the program. Training directors understand that applicants like to talk to their current interns and will be happy to arrange for you to talk to one of them.

You also should remember that *every* contact that you have with a site could potentially be a part of the interview process. Even your interactions with support staff—positive or negative—might find their way to the selection committee. Sometimes current interns are members of the selection committee, and thus your contacts with them might ultimately be a part of the interview process as well.

Question 16. What should I do if someone at an internship site violates the Match policies by asking me about how I intend to rank that site?

We hope that this won't happen to you, as most training directors are very careful and don't want to put internship applicants in such an uncomfortable position (nor do they want to get into trouble with APPIC!). But, if this does happen, the best approach is to politely remind the interviewer that the APPIC Match policies do not permit you to share such information with them. Of course, this can result in a brief uncomfortable moment in the interview and possibly some embarrassment on the part of the interviewer, but it can provide an important reminder to the interviewer about the policies. And, in most instances, the interviewer will gain respect for you for having the courage to appropriately set this boundary during an interview.

We have found that, most of the time, such policy violations are the result of mistakes, misunderstandings, or miscommunications among the training staff and are rarely intentional or malicious acts.

You should also remember that APPIC has both an informal problem resolution process and a formal complaint process that can be used to address violations of the Match policies. Thus, you should not hesitate to contact APPIC if you need assistance in resolving a difficult situation.

Question 17. What should I do if someone at an internship site asks me a question on an interview that is illegal?

According to an APPIC newsletter article by Mona Koppel Mitnick, Esq., an attorney and the public member of the APPIC Board of Directors, the following questions should not be asked of internship applicants unless they relate to actual qualifications for the position or the applicant raises the issue himself or herself: marital or family status, religion, physical condition or limitations, sexual preference, or physical or mental health status. This is not an exhaustive list, and there may be certain conditions in which some of these questions may be legally asked.

If you are asked such a question on an interview, there are a couple of ways to respond. One approach is to let the interviewer know that you are not comfortable answering the question or that you believe that it is not an appropriate question for an interview. However, we do recognize that some applicants may be hesitant to respond this way out of concern that it will lead to a negative response by the interviewer or that they will be seen as "resistant" or "uncooperative."

Another approach is to simply answer the question in the moment but to take some form of action at a later time. For example, you could later (either after the interview or after the entire selection process) contact the training director to inform him or her about the fact that you were asked a question that you believe may be illegal. Our belief is that most training directors will be grateful that you have brought this issue to their attention so that they can take corrective action with the individual involved.

Alternatively, you can use APPIC's informal problem resolution or formal complaint processes to address the situation. In particular, if you are unsure about the legality or appropriateness of a particular interview question, the informal problem resolution process can provide an opportunity for you to discuss the situation confidentially with an APPIC representative and review the options that might be available to you.

Also, keep in mind that there are some interview questions that you may consider to be "inappropriate" but that are legal nonetheless. A good example is, "Tell us about the other sites at which you have applied for an internship." Some applicants find this question to be somewhat intrusive and unnecessary, but there is nothing to prevent a site from asking it.

Additional resources on the topic of legal and illegal interview questions may be found at the APPIC Web site, http://www.appic.org.

THE MATCH *Question 18. When should I register for the Match? What happens if I register late and do not get my applicant code number in time to provide it to sites on the AAPI?*

We generally recommend that you register for the Match in September or early October to receive your applicant code number in time to put it on the AAPI. However, if you are unsure about whether or not you will be applying for internship in the coming year, you may wish to wait until closer to the deadline, as the Match registration fee is nonrefundable. If you register later in the process and do not receive your applicant code number in time to put it on your AAPI, do not worry—there will be plenty of time to provide your number to sites later in the process.

Question 19. Both my partner and I will be applying for psychology internships this year. Are there any special procedures that are available for us?

Any two applicants who wish to coordinate their choices of internship may participate in the Match as a "couple." Most couples will find it advantageous to use these special procedures to attempt to secure internships in the same geographic area. More information is available on the APPIC and NMS Web sites.

Question 20. What considerations do I use when constructing my rankings?

The most important thing to remember is to simply rank internship programs in the order in which *you* want them. That is all you need to worry about. Do not, under any circumstances, take into account such things as how you believe a site is ranking you, how well you think you have impressed a site, the feedback that you are getting from a site, and so forth. The Matching program has been specifically designed to allow you to rank sites in the order in which you want them, without consideration of these other factors, in order to be assured of receiving the best match possible.

Question 21. What if I do not know whether I am still under consideration by a site—should I still rank that site?

As long as you are still interested in the site, you should rank it. It does not hurt you in any way to rank a site that does not ultimately rank you. If that happens, the computer will simply skip over that site on your list and proceed with the next ranked site, without having reduced your chances of being matched to any other site on your list.

Question 22. I am hesitant to give up my top ranking to a site that does not seem all that interested in me.

This is an understandable concern. However, if a site is truly your top choice, then you should absolutely, positively rank that site as number 1 on your list regardless of how interested they seem in you. By doing so, you will not have reduced your chances of being matched to other sites on your list if your top-ranked site does not work out.

Question 23. I just received a letter today from one of my ranked sites saying I was no longer under consideration. But, I have already submitted my rankings! Any suggestions?

Do not worry. The computer will simply skip over that program on your list—it will not affect your chances of getting matched to any of your other sites. In other words, even if you did log in to the Rank Order List Input and Confirmation system to remove that program from your list, it would not matter—you would still be matched to the exact same program as if you left it on your list.

Question 24. Given my current circumstances, I am not completely sure that I want to attend internship during the coming year. Should I still submit a rank order list (ROL)?

You should submit a ROL only if you are absolutely, positively, 100% sure that you are ready to accept the internship to which you are matched. The APPIC Match is binding, and you are not permitted to change your mind once matched to an internship site. Thus, if you are unsure about your ability to commit to internship during the coming year, then you should not submit a ROL.

Question 25. What if I decide that I do not like the internship site to which I have been matched? Is it possible to change my mind?

No, you are required to attend the internship program to which you are matched.

Question 26. What is the first thing that I should do if I am not matched?

Talk to people. Talking to your significant others will give you the support you need and some guidance about how to proceed. Talking to your academic advisor and your DCT will help you identify the necessary steps to search for available internship slots that are acceptable to you and to important others in your life. The weekend before APPIC Match Day is the perfect time to have these discussions, as well as the time to prepare for the opening of the Clearinghouse. If you do decide to use the Clearinghouse, be sure to review the extensive instructions and suggestions for applicants located on the APPIC Web site.

Question 27. I think that a site may have violated an APPIC policy. I am uncertain if their behavior was really a violation, and even if it was, if I should risk reporting it. What should I do?

Probably the best approach is to discuss the situation with APPIC's Informal Problem Resolution consultant (see www.appic.org for contact information for this person). Your initial contact with this consultant will be to confidentially discuss the situation and is an opportunity for you to better understand your options for resolution of the problem. Contacting APPIC doesn't obligate you to take any action or to file a complaint.

The Match policies were put into place to make the internship application and match process one that is fair and respectful for students and sites alike. Although violations are uncommon, they do occur. Students often wonder if reporting a potential violation will have negative consequences for them or their chances of securing an internship. This is rarely the case. Your situation can be handled informally or formally, depending on the nature of your complaint. If the problem is serious, it is important for you to inform APPIC of the problem because one of their member-sites may not be complying with the rules they agreed to abide by.

Question 28. I have more questions that have not been addressed in this chapter. What do I do?

You have several options available. First, ask your DCT or other faculty members for assistance. Second, you may post your questions to the APPIC INTERN-NETWORK e-mail list (see Appendix A). This list is moderated by Dr. Greg Keilin, the APPIC Match Coordinator, and also has a number of training directors and previous years' applicants who monitor the list and can help answer your questions. You can also contact Dr. Keilin directly via e-mail or telephone, and he will be happy to assist you.

In addition, we would be very grateful if you would send along your question to Dr. Carol Williams-Nickelson at APA and APAGS (cwilliams-nickelson@apa.org) as your input might be valuable for future intern applicants, and we would be pleased to consider including your question in future editions of this workbook.

Appendix A

Additional Resources

Internship Workshops and Programs

APAGS offers many resources to assist students with internship-related issues. In addition to the annual APAGS Preconvention workshop, APAGS routinely offers other convention programming addressing different aspects of the internship process. For information about registration for these programs, visit the APAGS Web site (www. apa.org/apags). There are also opportunities for universities and programs to host an APAGS internship workshop on their campus presented by the APAGS Central Office staff and often by members of the APAGS Committee. For more information about this opportunity, contact the APAGS Central Office, (202) 336-6014.

APAGS Liaison to APPIC

APAGS works closely with APPIC by sending an APAGS member liaison to all APPIC meetings. The APAGS Web site and the APAGS magazine, *gradPSYCH*, features articles on the topic of internship.

APAGS Internship Listserv

APAGS sponsors a listserv for APAGS members who are preparing for and experiencing the internship application process. The list also serves as a forum for individuals currently on internship to discuss transition and career issues. All listserv subscribers may post questions to the list and contribute to the listserv discussion. APAGS members may subscribe to this list by sending the following message, with a blank subject line and your signature line disabled, to

> Listserv@lists.apa.org
> Subscribe APAGSINTERNSHIP First-Name Last-Name
> *Example:* Subscribe APAGSINTERNSHIP Terry Gradley

A Survival Guide for Ethnic Minority Graduate Students

APAGS members may obtain this publication by contacting APAGS directly or from the APAGS Web site's members-only page. This comprehensive guide is applicable for all students in content and includes sections on mentoring, networking, stress management and balance, impostor syndrome, racism, research, teaching, obtaining funding, comprehensive exams, dissertation management, internship, and professional development.

APAGS Web Site

Visit the APAGS Web site (www.apa.org/apags) to learn more about APAGS and the support and resources APAGS provides to its graduate student members. Information about joining APAGS is also available on the APAGS Web site.

APPIC RESOURCES

The APPIC Web Site

APPIC has extensive information about the Match and Clearinghouse, APPIC e-mail lists, informal and formal problem resolution, the AAPI, and many other important documents on it's Web site (http://www.appic.org). Students may be particularly interested in the following resources:

The MATCH-NEWS E-mail List

This free e-mail list provides up-to-date news and information about the APPIC Match. It is strongly recommended that internship applicants subscribe to this list as early as possible in the process. Subscribing to this list means that you will receive occasional e-mail messages (usually only a few per month) containing news, tips, and suggestions about how to make the most of the APPIC Match and the selection process. Only APPIC personnel are authorized to post messages to this list. To subscribe, send a blank e-mail message to subscribe-match-news@lyris.appic.org.

The INTERN-NETWORK E-mail List

This free e-mail list is intended for discussion of professional psychology internship issues among internship applicants and current interns. Many applicants use the INTERN-NETWORK list to ask questions or discuss issues related to the internship selection process. Some Training Directors and previous Match participants are subscribed to the list in order to assist the current year's applicants. This is an all-to-all discussion list, and any list subscriber may post messages to the list. To subscribe, send a blank e-mail message to subscribe-intern-network@lyris.appic.org.

The APPIC Directory

The APPIC Directory is provided as a service to students, graduate faculty, and training directors in identifying APPIC-member internship and post-doctoral training programs that are likely to meet specific training needs. The APPIC Directory is available in both printed and electronic forms. The printed version of the Directory is issued once each year (usually in June) and may be purchased directly from the APPIC Central Office. The electronic version of the Directory (the "APPIC Directory Online") provides more information about each program than does the printed version of the Directory and provides a number of search options that allow users to quickly identify programs of interest. Visit http://www.appic.org to access the Directory Online.

The National Matching Services Web site

The APPIC Internship Matching Program is administered on behalf of APPIC by National Matching Services, Inc. (NMS). Registration materials for the APPIC Match may be downloaded from this site. Applicants will find extensive information about the APPIC Match on the NMS Web site at http://www.natmatch.com/psychint/.

PUBLICATIONS   Brown, R. T. (1996). Training in professional psychology: Are we addressing the issues? *Professional Psychology: Research and Practice, 27,* 506–507.

Constantine, M .G., & Keilin, W. G. (1996). Association of Postdoctoral and Internship Centers' guidelines and the internship selection process: A survey of applicants and academic and internship training directors. *Professional Psychology: Research and Practice, 27,* 308–314.

Constantine, M. G., Keilin, W. C., Litwinowicz, J., & Romanus, T. (1997). Postnotification day perceptions of unplaced internship applicants and their academic training directors: Recommendations for improving future internship selection processes. *Professional Psychology: Research and Practice, 28,* 387–392.

Holaday, M., & McPhearson, R. (1996). Standardization of the APPIC predoctoral internship application forms. *Professional Psychology: Research and Practice, 27,* 508–513.

Keilin, W. G. (1998). Internship selection 30 years later: An overview of the APPIC matching program. *Professional Psychology: Research and Practice, 29,* 599–603.

Keilin, W. G. (2000). Internship selection in 1999: Was the Association of Psychology Postdoctoral and Internship Centers' match a success? *Professional Psychology: Research and Practice, 31,* 281–287.

Keilin, W. G., Thorn, E. E., Rodolfa, E. R., Constantine, M. G., & Kaslow, N. J. (2000). Examining the balance of internship supply and demand: 1999 Association of Psychology Postdoctoral and Internship Centers' match implications. *Professional Psychology: Research and Practice, 31,* 288–294.

Lopez, S. J., & Draper, P. K. (1997). Recent developments and more internship tips: A comment on Mellott, Arden, and Cho (1997). *Professional Psychology: Research and Practice, 28,* 496–498.

Lopez, S. J., & Edwardson, T. (1996). Quantifying practicum experience: A comment on Hecker, Fink, Levasseur, and Parker (1995). *Professional Psychology: Research and Practice, 27,* 514–517.

Lopez, S. J., Ochlert, M. E., & Moberly, R. L. (1996). Selection criteria for American Psychological Association-accredited internship programs: A survey of training directors. *Professional Psychology: Research and Practice, 27,* 518–520.

Mellott, R. N., Arden, I. A., & Cho, M. E. (1997). Preparing for internship: Tips for the prospective applicant. *Professional Psychology: Research and Practice, 28,* 190–196.

Mitchell, S. L. (1996). Getting a foot in the door: The written internship application. *Professional Psychology: Research and Practice, 27,* 90–92.

Oehlert, M. E., Lopez, S. J., & Sumerall, S. W. (1997). Internship application: Increased costs accompany increased competitiveness. *Professional Psychology: Research and Practice, 28,* 595–596.

Prinstein, M. J., & Patterson, M. D. (2004). *The portable mentor: Expert guide to a successful career in psychology.* New York: Kluwer Academic/Plenum.

Stewart, A. E., & Stewart, E. A. (1996a). A decision-making technique for choosing a psychology internship. *Professional Psychology: Research and Practice, 27,* 521–526.

Stewart, A. E., & Stewart, E. A. (1996b). Personal and practical considerations in selecting a psychology internship. *Professional Psychology: Research and Practice, 27,* 295–303.

Appendix B

The AAPI

Please note: The APPIC application as it appears in this book is valid only for the year it is dated. APPIC reserves the right to revise the AAPI at any time and urges users to check the APPIC Web site for the current version. APPIC is not liable for any errors or omissions in the AAPI as it appears in this book.

INSTRUCTIONS
APPIC APPLICATION FOR PSYCHOLOGY INTERNSHIP (AAPI)
2003-2004

Revised June 23, 2003

This application was created with input from APPIC Member internships and APPIC Subscriber doctoral programs in the United States and Canada. The data requested is comprehensive, but *there is no expectation that an intern applicant would have had all the experiences listed, administered all of the assessment instruments, or be licensed as a mental health practitioner.*

This 2003-2004 AAPI is formatted so that it may be completed on a computer. Some internship sites may request that you send them only certain sections of the AAPI, and some may require additional site-specific information from you to supplement the AAPI.

Please direct any questions about the AAPI to Dr. Joyce Illfelder-Kaye at jxi1@psu.edu (note this e-mail address has the letters "jxi" followed by the number "1"). **You might also check out the APPIC website at www.appic.org to see if the answer to your question is included in the section on Frequently Asked Questions Regarding the AAPI.**

Instructions:

1. This version of the AAPI is valid through April 30, 2004, and should be used only to apply for internship positions that begin in 2004.
2. This AAPI document consists of TWO PARTS: (1) AAPI Part 1, divided into six sections, to be completed by the applicant; and (2) AAPI Part 2 - the Academic Program's Verification of Internship Eligibility and Readiness Form - to be completed by the applicant and the academic training director.
3. The "@" (at-sign) character has been used to designate the places in which you need to enter information. Simply use your word processor to replace each "@" character with the appropriate information.
   Some questions will provide a list of answers, each preceded by a "@", and will instruct you to "put an X next to one choice." To respond to these questions,

replace the "@" next to your answer with an "X", and change all other "@" symbols to blank spaces.

4. Please ensure that each of the six sections of the AAPI begins on a separate page. At any point, if you require more space to answer a question than is allotted, feel free to create the additional space needed.

5. It is strongly recommended that you save your work often, using the "Save" command in your word processor.

6. Before submitting Part 1 of the AAPI to an internship site, be sure that you sign and date the application in Section 6. Remember to remove this "instructions" page before submitting. Please do not delete other instructions in the body of the AAPI as readers become familiar with the placement of items.

7. Part 2 of the AAPI, the Academic Program's Verification of Internship Eligibility and Readiness Form, should be printed separately and completed by both the applicant and his/her Training Director (please see the instructions for that form). It is acceptable to APPIC to submit photocopies of this form with the signature photocopied. Please consult the application instructions for each site for more information in the event that this is not acceptable to a specific site.

8. Please be aware that this is a universal application. Sites will not expect you to have experiences in all areas covered by the AAPI. Different types of sites will emphasize different types of experiences in order to ascertain fit with their program.

PART 1

Participants in the APPIC Match, including applicants and internship programs, may not communicate, solicit, accept, or use any ranking-related information prior to the release of the Match results.

Application Date: @

SECTION 1: BACKGROUND AND EDUCATIONAL INFORMATION

A. BACKGROUND

1. **Name:** @

2. **Social Security No. or**
   Social Insurance No.: @
   (Optional, recommended if applying to a federal agency, e.g. VA, Federal Bureau of Prisons)

3. **Match I.D. Number:** @
   (Please note: If you do not have your match ID number at this time, you may provide it to internship sites at a later date, once you receive it from National Matching Services.)

4. **Home Address:** @
   @
   @

5. **Work Address:** @
   @
   @

6. **Phone (Home):** @
7. **Phone (Work):** @
8. **FAX:** @
9. **E-Mail:** @

10. **What is your country of citizenship?** (put an "X" next to one choice)
    @ U.S.
    @ Canada
    @ Other (Specify: @)

11. **Non-citizen visa status:** @
12. **Is this visa current and valid?** @

13. **Does this visa permit you to work?**   @

(If you are applying to another country, you may need to begin the process of researching these issues now.)

14. **Are you a veteran?**   @

15. **On APPIC Match Day, many Internship Training Directors will call the applicants with whom they have been matched.** Please specify the phone number where you may be reached between 11:00 AM and 1:00 PM ET on that day.

@

B. <u>EDUCATION</u>

<u>Current Academic Work</u>

1. **What is the name and address of the university/institution in which your graduate department is located?**

@
@
@

2. **What is the name of your department?** (e.g. Department of Psychology, Division of Behavioral Foundations in Educational Psychology)?

@

3. **What is the name of your graduate program?** This will likely be the same as or similar to the subfield of your degree (see the next question) but it could be different (e.g. Clinical, School, etc.)

@

4. **What is the designated subfield of your doctorate in Psychology?** (Put an "X" next to only one choice):

@ Clinical (adult track)   @ Health
@ Clinical (child track)   @ Neuropsychology
@ Clinical (general)   @ School
@ Counseling   @ Respecialization Program
@ Developmental   @ Combined (Specify: @)
@ Educational   @ Other (Specify: @)

5. **What is your primary theoretical orientation?** (Put an "X" next to only one choice)

@ Behavioral
@ Biological
@ Cognitive Behavioral
@ Eclectic
@ Humanistic/Existential

@ Integrative
@ Interpersonal
@ Psychodynamic/Psychoanalytic
@ Systems
@ Other (Specify: @)

6. **What degree are you seeking?** (Put an "X" next to only one choice)

@ Ph.D.
@ Psy.D.
@ Ed.D.
@ Ph.D./J.D.
@ Certificate/Respecialization (Specify: @)
@ Other (Specify: @)

7. **Name of Training Director:** @
8. **Training Director E-Mail:** @
9. **University / School Phone #:** @
10. **University / School Fax #:** @

11. **What is the status of your doctoral training program?** (Put an "X" next to all that apply):

@ APA-Accredited
@ APA-Accredited, on probation
@ Not Accredited

@ CPA-Accredited
@ CPA-Accredited, on probation

12. **If not APA / CPA-accredited, is the school regionally accredited?**

@ Yes
@ No

13. **What is your Department's Training Model** (ask your Training Director if unsure):

@ Clinical Scientist
@ Scientist-Practitioner
@ Other - specify: @
(e.g. Developmental, Specialty, Local Clinical Scientist)

@ Practitioner-Scholar
@ Practitioner

14. **When did you begin graduate level study in your current program?** If you received your baccalaureate from the same department provide the date on which you started **GRADUATE** work (e.g., a start date of January, 1996 in the graduate program would be 01 / 1996.). **DO INCLUDE** any master's work that preceded or counted toward the doctoral degree, **IF IN THE SAME PROGRAM.**

@ / @ (mm / yyyy)

15. **When did you complete (or do you expect to complete) your doctoral course-work, excluding dissertation and internship hours (if applicable)?**

    @ / @ (mm / yyyy)

16. **Have you successfully completed your program's comprehensive / qualifying examination?** (Put an "X" next to only one choice).

    @   Yes - Date of completion: @ / @ (mm / yyyy)
    @   No
    @   Not applicable

17. **What is your dissertation / research title or topic?**

    @

18. **What type of research is involved in question 17 above?** (Put an "X" next to only one choice)

    @   Critical literature review / theoretical
    @   Original data collection
    @   Use of existing database
    @   Other (Specify: @)

19. **What is the current status of your dissertation / doctoral research project?** (Please indicate the date, in mm/yyyy format, that each of the following was completed or is expected to be completed; if not applicable, instead enter "Not Applicable"):

	Date Completed or Expected (mm / yyyy)
Proposal approved	@ / @
Data collected	@ / @
Data analyzed	@ / @
Defended	@ / @

20. **If no dissertation is required, describe the status of any major project (if applicable):**

    @

21. **Name of dissertation / doctoral research advisor:**   @
22. **Phone Number:**   @
23. **E-Mail:**   @

Previous Academic Work

24. **What is the highest degree that you have completed in any mental health field?**

   @   Ph.D.
   @   Psy.D.
   @   Ed.D.
   @   M.S.W.
   @   M.A. / M.S.
   @   B.S.W.
   @   B.A. / B.S.
   @   Ed.S.
   @   Other (Specify: @)

25. **When did you complete the above degree?** (Do not respond to this item if this is an undergraduate degree.)

   @ / @ (mm / yyyy)

26. **Please complete the following table for each undergraduate school attended:** (list in chronological order).

School / University	Major	Degree Earned	GPA
@	@	@	@

27. **Please complete the following table for each graduate school or university attended:** (list in chronological order)

School / University	Major	Degree Earned	Dates of Attendance	GPA
@	@	@	@	@

28. **Licensure / Certification:** Some applicants may be licensed or certified at the master's level. If you are, please list any current and valid licenses or certifications in mental health fields (list type and jurisdiction, e.g., state or province):

   @

29. **Please list any honors received:**

   @

30. **Please list names, addresses, phone numbers, and e-mail addresses of individuals who will be forwarding letters of recommendation:**

   @

SECTION 2: ESSAYS

Instructions: Please answer each question in 500 words or less.

1. **Please provide an autobiographical statement.** (There is <u>no</u> "correct" format for this question. Answer this question as if someone had asked you, "tell me something about yourself." It is an opportunity for you to provide the internship site with some information about yourself. It is entirely up to you to decide what information you wish to provide along with the format in which to present it.)

    @

2. **Please describe your theoretical orientation and how this influences your approach to case conceptualization and intervention. You may use de-identified case material to illustrate your points if you choose.**

    @

3. **Please describe your experience and training in work with diverse populations. Your discussion should display explicitly the manner in which multicultural / diversity issues influence your clinical practice and case conceptualization.**

    @

4. **Please describe your research experience and interests.**

    @

5. **How do you envision our internship site meeting your training goals and interests?** (Note: this question requires you to address site-specific issues and training opportunities; thus, you may wish to submit different responses to different sites. If you are addressing these issues in a cover letter, please feel free to refer the reader to the cover letter and do not repeat here).

    @

SECTION 3: DOCTORAL PRACTICUM DOCUMENTATION

This form was created to allow applicants to document their experience in therapy and other psychological interventions. While this form lists a wide range of experiences that one might have had, **no applicant is expected to have experience in all, or even most, of these areas.** In fact, most internship programs focus on those areas that are a good fit for their program. You are advised to identify those categories that fit best with your experiences and provide the relevant information for those categories.

INSTRUCTIONS FOR THIS SECTION:

1. For items 1 - 6 in this section, you should only count hours for which you received formal academic training and credit or which were program-sanctioned training experiences (e.g., VA summer traineeship, clinical research positions). Practicum hours must be supervised. Please consult with your academic training director to determine whether experiences are considered program sanctioned or not.

2. You will be asked to report your practicum hours separately for: (1) practicum hours accrued in your doctoral program, and (2) practicum hours accrued as part of a terminal master's experience in a mental health field. **Hours accrued while earning a master's degree as part of a doctoral program should be counted as doctoral practicum hours.**

3. **Practicum hour** - A practicum hour is a clock hour, not a semester / quarter hour. A 45-50 minute client / patient hour may be counted as one practicum hour.

4. Items 1 - 3 below are meant to be mutually exclusive; thus, any practicum hour should **not** be counted more than once across these three items. **You may have some experiences that could potentially fall under more than one category, but it is your responsibility to select the category that you feel best captures the experience.** (For example, a Stress Management group might be classified as a group or as a Medical / Health-Related Intervention, but not both.)

5. For items 1 - 3, include only experience accrued through November 1, 2003. Item 4 will allow you to designate estimated future practicum hours to be accrued prior to the start of internship.

6. When calculating practicum hours, you should provide your <u>best estimate</u> of hours accrued or number of clients / patients seen. It is understood that you may not have the exact numbers available. Please round to the nearest whole number. Use your best judgment, in consultation with your academic training director, in quantifying your practicum experience.

1. **INTERVENTION AND ASSESSMENT EXPERIENCE - How much experience do you have with different types of psychological interventions and assessment?**

Please report actual clock hours in direct service to clients / patients. Hours should not be counted in more than one category. Time spent gathering information about the client / patient, but not in the actual presence of the client / patient, should instead be recorded under item 2, below ("Support Activities").

For the "Total hours face-to-face" columns, count each hour of a group, family, or couples session as one practicum hour. For example, a two-hour group session with 12 adults is counted as two hours. For the "# of different. . ." columns, count a couple, family, or group as one (1) unit. For example, meeting with a group of 12 adults over a ten-week period counts as one (1) group. Groups may be closed or open membership; but, in either case, count the group as one group.

	DOCTORAL		MASTERS	

a. Individual Therapy

	Total hours face-to-face	# of different individuals	Total hours face-to-face	# of different individuals
1) Older Adults (65+)	@	@	@	@
2) Adults (18-64)	@	@	@	@
3) Adolescents (13-17)	@	@	@	@
4) School-Age (6-12)	@	@	@	@
5) Pre-School Age (3-5)	@	@	@	@
6) Infants / Toddlers (0-2)	@	@	@	@

b. Career Counseling

1) Adults	@	@	@	@
2) Adolescents	@	@	@	@

c. Group Therapy

	Total hours face-to-face	# of different groups	Total hours face-to-face	# of different groups
1) Adults	@	@	@	@
2) Adolescents (13-17)	@	@	@	@
3) Children (12 and under)	@	@	@	@

d. Family Therapy

	Total hours face-to-face	# of different families	Total hours face-to-face	# of different families
	@	@	@	@

e. Couples Therapy

	Total hours face-to-face	# of different couples	Total hours face-to-face	# of different couples
	@	@	@	@

f. School Counseling Interventions

	Total hours face-to-face	# of different individuals	Total hours face-to-face	# of different individuals
1) Consultation	@	@	@	@
2) Direct Intervention	@	@	@	@
3) Other (Specify: @)	@	@	@	@

g. Other Psychological Interventions

1) Sports Psychology / Performance Enhancement	@	@	@	@
2) Medical / Health - Related Interventions	@	@	@	@
3) Intake Interview / Structured Interview	@	@	@	@
4) Substance Abuse Interventions	@	@	@	@
5) Other interventions (e.g., milieu therapy, treatment planning with the patient present.)	@	@	@	@

Please describe the nature of the experience(s) listed in g-5:

@

h. Psychological Assessment Experience

Psychological Assessment Experience: This is the estimated total number of face to face client contact hours administering and providing feedback to clients/patients. This does not include time spent scoring and/or report writing, which should be included under item 2, below ("Support Activities"). You will provide information about numbers of tests administered in Section 4 of the AAPI.

	DOCTORAL Total hours face-to-face	MASTERS Total hours face-to-face
1) Psychodiagnostic test administration (Include symptom assessment, projectives, personality, objective measures, achievement, intelligence, and career assessment), and providing feedback to clients/patients.	@	@
2) Neuropsychological Assessment (Include intellectual assessment in this category only when it was administered in the context of neuropsychological assessment involving evaluation of multiple cognitive, sensory and motor functions).	@	@

i. Other Psychological Experience with Students and/or Organizations:

	DOCTORAL Total hours face-to-face	MASTERS Total hours face-to-face
1) Supervision of other students performing intervention and assessment activities	@	@
2) Program Development/Outreach Programming	@	@
3) Outcome Assessment of programs or projects	@	@
4) Systems Intervention / Organizational Consultation / Performance Improvement	@	@
5) Other (Specify: @)	@	@

TOTAL INTERVENTION AND ASSESSMENT HOURS:

Add the number of hours included
in 1a through 1i above

	DOCTORAL Total hours face-to-face	**MASTERS** Total hours face-to-face
Total Intervention & Assessment Hours:	@	@

2. **SUPPORT ACTIVITIES–How much time have you spent in support activities related to your intervention and assessment experience?** This item includes activities spent outside the counseling / therapy hour while still focused on the client / patient (e.g. chart review, writing process notes, consulting with other professionals about cases, video / audio tape review, time spent planning interventions, assessment interpretation and report writing, etc.). In addition, it includes hours spent at a practicum setting in didactic training (e.g. grand rounds, seminars).

	DOCTORAL Total hours	**MASTERS** Total hours
Total Support Hours:	@	@

3. **SUPERVISION RECEIVED–How much time have you spent in supervision?** Supervision is divided into one-to-one, group, and peer supervision / consultation. Supervision provided to less advanced students should be counted in item 1i-1, above.

   Item 3a: Hours are defined as regularly scheduled, face-to-face individual supervision with specific intent of overseeing the psychological services rendered by the student.

   Items 3b and 3c: The hours recorded in the group supervision category should be actual hours of group focus on specific cases. Many excellent practicum courses incorporate both didactic and experiential components in the course activity. **While the didactic portion is excellent training, it should not be recorded as a supervision activity; it should instead be included as a support activity in Item 2 ("Support Activities") above.** This may necessitate breaking the hours spent in a practicum course into intervention, supervision, and didactic activities by actual course hours. For example, if you present on the "Psychosocial Issues of HIV Infection" using examples of cases, it is a didactic activity. Similarly, Grand Rounds that consists of in-service education on specific topics would <u>not</u> be considered supervision for the purposes of documenting practicum hours, but would be considered a support activity.

		DOCTORAL Total hours	**MASTERS** Total hours
a.	Hours spent in one-on-one, face-to-face supervision:	@	@
b.	Hours spent in group supervision:	@	@
c.	Hours of peer supervision / consultation and case discussion on specific cases:	@	@
Total Supervision Hours (add 3a, 3b, and 3c):		@	@

4. **SUMMARY OF PRACTICUM HOURS** - This section summarizes the total number of practicum hours described above, along with estimated future practicum hours. In columns one and two, please include the total hours as designated in items 1 - 3 above. In column three, please estimate the number of hours to be accrued between November 2, 2003 and July 1, 2004.

	Doctoral through Nov. 1, 2003	Masters	Estimated after Nov. 1, 2003
a. Total Intervention and Assessment Hours (item 1):	@	@	@
b. Total Support Hours (item 2):	@	@	@
c. Total Supervision Hours (item 3):	@	@	@
GRAND TOTAL	@	@	@

5. **TREATMENT SETTINGS - How many practicum hours have you spent in each of the following treatment settings?** Please indicate the estimated <u>total number</u> of practicum hours (including intervention and assessment, support, and supervision) spent in each of the following treatment settings through November 1, 2003. The total number of practicum hours for this section should equal the Grand Total in item 4, columns 1 and 2, above.

	DOCTORAL Total hours	MASTERS Total hours
Child Guidance Clinic	@	@
Community Mental Health Center	@	@
Department Clinic (psychology clinic run by a department or school)	@	@
Forensic / Justice setting (e.g., jail, prison)	@	@
Inpatient Hospital	@	@
Military	@	@
Outpatient Medical / Psychiatric Clinic & Hospital	@	@
University Counseling Center / Student Mental Health Center	@	@
Schools	@	@
Other (Specify: @)	@	@
Total Hours in all Treatment Settings	@	@

6. **OTHER INFORMATION ABOUT YOUR PRACTICUM OR WORK EXPERIENCE:**

a. What types of groups have you led or co-led? Please describe.

   @

b. Do you have experience with Managed Care Providers in a professional therapy / counseling / assessment capacity? (Put an "X" next to only one choice)

   @ Yes
   @ No

c. Have you audio or videotaped clients/patients and reviewed these tapes with your clinical supervisor?

   Audio tape review

   @ Yes
   @ No

   Videotape review

   @ Yes
   @ No

d. In which languages other than English (including American Sign Language), are you FLUENT enough to conduct therapy?

   @

e. What is your experience with diverse populations in a professional therapy / counseling capacity? Please indicate the number of clients/patients seen for each of the following diverse populations. You may provide additional information or comments in the space provided. Include clients/patients for whom you performed assessments or intake interviews. For this item, you may include a single client/patient in more than one category, as appropriate. For families and/or couples, please count each individual separately.

Race / Ethnicity	Number of Different Clients / Patients Seen
African-American / Black / African Origin	@
Asian-American / Asian Origin / Pacific Islander	@
Latino-a / Hispanic	@
American Indian / Alaska Native / Aboriginal Canadian	@
European Origin / White	@
Bi-racial / Multi-racial	@
Other (specify below)	@

@

<u>Sexual Orientation</u> (Please indicate only for those clients where this information is known.)

Heterosexual @

Gay @

Lesbian @

Bisexual @

Other (specify below) @
@

<u>Disabilities</u>

Physical / Orthopedic Disability @

Blind / Visually Impaired @

Deaf / Hard of Hearing @

Learning / Cognitive Disability @

Developmental Disability @

Serious Mental Illness (e.g., primary psychotic disorders, @
major mood disorders that significantly interfere with
adaptive functioning, severe developmental disabilities)

Other (specify below) @
@

<u>Gender</u>

Male @

Female @

Transgendered @

<u>Comments</u>:
@

7. **TEACHING EXPERIENCES - What is your teaching experience?** Please summarize any teaching experience that you have. Include both undergraduate and graduate courses taught.

@

8. **CLINICAL WORK EXPERIENCES–What other clinical experiences have you had?** Some students may have had work experience outside of their master's and doctoral training. This section is to include professional work experiences separate from practica or program sanctioned work experience. Use this section to describe settings and activities that are not included in items 1-7 above, "Intervention and Assessment Experience". You may simply provide this information in narrative form or you may present this information in a format similar to that used above (i.e., using the format from one or more items 1-7 above). If you choose to identify hours, please use the same criteria for intervention and assessment hours, support hours, and supervision hours.

@

SECTION 4: TEST ADMINISTRATION

What is your experience with the following instruments? Please indicate all instruments used by you in your assessment experience, excluding practice administrations to fellow students. You may include any experience you have had with these instruments such as work, research, practicum, etc., other than practice administrations. Please indicate the number of tests that you administered and scored in the first column, and the number that you administered, scored, interpreted and wrote a report for in the second column. Please designate your experiences for the instruments listed below, <u>without changing the sequence in which they are listed</u>. Then, you may add as many additional lines (under "Other Tests") as needed for any other tests that you have administered.

1. ADULT TESTS

Name of Test	# Administered and Scored	# of Reports Written
Bender Gestalt	@	@
Millon Clinical Multi-Axial Inv. III (MCMI)	@	@
MMPI-II	@	@
Myers-Briggs Type Indicator	@	@
Personality Assessment Inventory	@	@
Projective Sentences (includes Rotter Sentence Completion and other Sentence Completion Tests)	@	@
Projective Drawings (includes Draw-a-Person Test and Kinetic Family Drawing Test)	@	@
Rorschach (scoring system: @)	@	@
Self-report measures of symptoms / disorders (e.g., Beck Depression Inventory)	@	@
Strong Interest Inventory	@	@
Structured Diagnostic Interviews (e.g., SADS, DIS)	@	@
TAT	@	@
Trail Making Test A & B	@	@
WAIS-III	@	@
Wechsler Memory Scale III	@	@

<u>Other Tests:</u>

	# Administered and Scored	# of Reports Written
@	@	@

2. CHILD AND ADOLESCENT TESTS

Name of Test	# Administered and Scored	# of Reports Written
Connors Scales (ADD assessment)	@	@
Diagnostic Interviews (e.g., DISC, Kiddie-SADS)	@	@
MMPI-A	@	@
Parent Report Measures (e.g., Child Behavior Checklist)	@	@
Peabody Picture Vocabulary Test	@	@
Rorschach (scoring system: @)	@	@
Self report measures of symptoms / disorders (e.g., Children's Depression Inventory)	@	@

WISC-III   @   @
WPPSI-R   @   @
WRAT   @   @

<u>Other Tests</u>:

@   @   @

3. INTEGRATED REPORT WRITING

How many supervised integrated psychological reports have you written for each of the following populations? An integrated report includes a history, an interview, and at least two tests from one or more of the following categories: personality assessments (objective and/or projective), intellectual assessment, cognitive assessment, and/or neuropsychological assessment. These are synthesized into a comprehensive report providing an overall picture of the patient.

a. Adults: @
b. Children / Adolescents: @

SECTION 5: PROFESSIONAL CONDUCT

Please answer ALL of the following questions with "YES" or "NO": (If yes, please elaborate)

1. Has disciplinary action, in writing, of any sort ever been taken against you by a supervisor, educational or training institution, health care institution, professional association, or licensing / certification board?

   @

2. Are there any complaints currently pending against you before any of the above bodies?

   @

3. Has there ever been a decision in a civil suit rendered against you relative to your professional work, or is any such action pending?

   @

4. Have you ever been suspended, terminated, or asked to resign by a graduate or internship training program, practicum site, or employer?

   @

5. Have you ever reneged on an APPIC internship match agreement (i.e., refused to attend or left an internship program that you obtained through the APPIC Match or Clearinghouse) without prior approval from APPIC and/or the internship site?

   @

6. Have you ever, in your lifetime, been convicted of an offense against the law other than a minor traffic violation?

   @

7. Have you ever, in your lifetime, been convicted of a felony?

   @

SECTION 6: APPLICATION CERTIFICATION

I certify that all of the information submitted by me in this application is true to the best of my knowledge and belief. I understand that any significant misstatement in, or omission from, this application may be cause for denial of selection as an intern or dismissal from an intern position. I authorize the internship site to consult with persons and institutions with which I have been associated who may have information bearing on my professional competence, character, and ethical qualifications now or in the future. I release from liability all internship staff for acts performed in good faith and without malice in connection with evaluating my application and my credentials and qualifications. I also release from liability all individuals and organizations who provide information to the internship site in good faith and without malice concerning my professional competence, ethics, character, and other qualifications now or in the future.

If I am accepted and become an intern, I expressly agree to comply fully with the Association of Psychology Postdoctoral and Internship Centers (APPIC) policies, the Ethical Principles of Psychologists and Code of Conduct and the General Guidelines for Providers of Psychological Services of the American Psychological Association, and with the standards of the Canadian Psychological Association which are applicable. I also agree to comply with all applicable state, provincial and federal laws, all of the Rules and Code of Conduct of the State or Provincial Licensing Board of Psychology, and the rules of the institution in which I am an intern.

I understand and agree that, as an applicant for the psychology internship program, I have the burden of producing adequate information for proper evaluation of my professional competence, character, ethics, and other qualifications and for resolving any doubts about such qualifications.

Applicant's Signature: Date:

APPIC APPLICATION FOR PSYCHOLOGY INTERNSHIP (AAPI)
2003-2004

PART 2
Academic Program's Verification of Internship Eligibility and Readiness

NOTE: This form is to be completed and submitted separately from Part 1 of the AAPI.

Instructions to the Applicant: In consultation with your graduate school training director, please complete questions 1 - 7 on your word processor. Please do not complete questions 8 - 15. You should then print out a copy of this form and provide it to your graduate school training director along with instructions about how this form is to be submitted to internship sites (some sites' materials will describe their requirements for submission). **It is acceptable to APPIC to submit photocopies of this form with the signature photocopied. However, please consult the application instructions for each site for more information, in the event that this is not acceptable to a specific site.**

Instructions to the Training Director: *It is your responsibility to ensure that the information on this form is accurate.* Please review and verify the information filled in by the applicant for questions 1 - 7 (and correct it, if necessary), complete questions 8 - 15, and sign and date this form. This form may either: (a) be sent directly to the internship site by you, or (b) be returned to the applicant (to be sent to the internship site by the applicant along with the AAPI and any other application materials). **It is acceptable to APPIC to submit photocopies of this form with the signature photocopied. The applicant should consult the application instructions for each site for more information in the event that this is not acceptable to a specific site. It is their responsibility to inform you of any exceptions.**

1. **Applicant's Name:**   @

2. **Doctoral Program / Department:**   @

3. **University / School:**   @

4. **Director of Training:**   @

5. **Director of Training's**   @
    Address, Phone, and E-Mail: @
                                              @
                                              @

6. **Academic Requirements**: It is understood that many applicants may still have comprehensive exams to complete prior to February 1, 2004 and coursework to complete prior to June 30, 2004. Please enter the dates that the following items were completed. Also, please list any requirements, as of today's date, that must still be completed before the student will be ready to go on internship, along with the expected date of completion.

In Column 1, enter the date completed or the expected completion date in mm/ yyyy format. If not applicable, instead enter "Not Applicable."

In Column 2, indicate with a "Yes" or "No" if the completion of the task is required by your program for a student to be able to <u>accept</u> an internship.

In Column 3, indicate with a "Yes" or "No" if the completion of the task is required by your program for a student to be able to <u>attend</u> an internship.

		Date Completed or Expected (mm / yyyy)	Required to accept an internship?	Required to attend an internship?
a.	Comprehensive / Qualifying Exam / Task	@ / @	@	@
b.	Academic Coursework *(excluding dissertation and internship hours if applicable)*	@ / @	@	@
c.	Master's Thesis	@ / @	@	@
d.	Dissertation / Doctoral Research Project			
	Proposal approved	@ / @	@	@
	Data collected	@ / @	@	@
	Data analyzed	@ / @	@	@
	Defended	@ / @	@	@

7. **Practicum Hours:** The above-named applicant has completed the following practicum hours as of November 1, 2003 (the hours listed below should be identical to the hours listed in Section 3 of the AAPI, item 4) (It is understood that the Training Director is verifying only experience that took place in the context of your program).

		Doctoral through Nov. 1, 2003	Masters	Estimated after Nov. 1, 2003
a.	Total Intervention and Assessment Hours (item 1):	@	@	@
b.	Total Support Hours (item 2):	@	@	@
c.	Total Supervision Hours (item 3):	@	@	@
	GRAND TOTAL	@	@	@

8. **Academic Standing:** Please answer the following questions regarding the above named student's academic standing. *This item is to be completed by the Training Director.*

a. Is this student in good standing?   Yes   No
    If no, please explain:

b. Is this student currently on probation?   Yes   No
    If yes, please explain:

c. Are any complaints currently pending against this student   Yes   No
    or were any filed in the past and found to be legitimate?
    If yes, please explain:

9. **Department's Training Model:** (Please circle) *This item is to be completed by the Training Director.*

      Clinical Scientist   Practitioner-Scholar

      Scientist-Practitioner   Practitioner

      Other - please specify:
        (e.g., Developmental, Specialty,
        Local Clinical Scientist)

10. **APA / CPA Accreditation:** (Please circle) *This item is to be completed by the Training Director.*

      Accredited

      Accredited, on Probation

      Not Accredited

11. Has this student ever reneged on an APPIC internship match agreement (i.e., refused to attend or left an internship program that was obtained through the APPIC Match or Clearinghouse) without prior approval from APPIC and/or the internship site? *This item is to be completed by the Training Director.*

      Yes   No

      If yes, please explain:

12. **Evaluation of Applicant:** Please answer the following statements. If you do not have sufficient information to rate the applicant, please check with other faculty, supervisors, etc. in order to complete this section. *This item is to be completed by the Training Director.*

a) This applicant possesses the emotional stability and   Yes   No
    maturity to handle the challenges of the internship
    experience.
b) This applicant possesses the theoretical / academic   Yes   No
    foundation necessary for effective counseling /
    clinical work.

c)	This applicant possesses the skills necessary for translating theory into integrated practice.	Yes	No
d)	This applicant demonstrates awareness of, and practices according to, the current ethical guidelines for psychologists.	Yes	No
e)	This applicant demonstrates the capacity to participate in supervision constructively and can modify his / her behavior in response to feedback.	Yes	No

13. **Additional comments:** Please identify areas of particular strength and areas in which the student needs further development. If you do not have direct knowledge of this student, please gather the appropriate information from relevant parties. *This item* **must** *be completed by the Training Director.* (If you are referring to an attached letter, please be sure that the letter addresses particular strengths and areas in which the student needs further development.)

14. **The faculty agrees that this student is ready to apply for internship.** (Please circle) *This item is to be completed by the Training Director.*

     Yes   No

If no, please explain:

15. **Once the student is on internship:** Who will serve as the contact person between your department and the internship program? (e.g., Training Director, Academic Advisor) *This item is to be completed by the Training Director.*

Name:

Work Address:

Phone:

E-Mail:

Signature of the Director of Training: _____

Date signed: _____

ABOUT THE EDITORS
AND CONTRIBUTORS

Carol Williams-Nickelson, PsyD, earned her degree from Our Lady of the Lake University in San Antonio and completed her predoctoral internship at the University of Notre Dame Counseling Center. She is the American Psychological Association's (APA's) associate executive director of the American Psychological Association of Graduate Students (APAGS) in Washington, DC. As APAGS' chief executive she is responsible for the overall development and management of all activities, projects, initiatives, convention programming, budgets, plans, and operations for the leaders and 45,000+ student members of APAGS. Currently, and as a former chair of APAGS, she serves as a spokesperson and advocate for graduate students to various psychology credentialing, accrediting, educational, training, and governing boards. She has presented many student and practitioner-oriented programs at APA Conventions and other professional meetings. Her research and publications focus on women's issues, stress and life-balance, entrepreneurialism, and leadership development.

Mitchell J. Prinstein, PhD, completed his doctoral degree at the University of Miami and his internship and postdoctoral fellowship at the Brown University School of Medicine. He is currently an associate professor and the director of clinical training in the Department of Psychology at Yale University and an adjunct assistant professor (research) at Brown. Dr. Prinstein's developmental psychopathology research examines interpersonal models of internalizing symptoms and health risk behaviors. He was first invited to speak about the internship application process in 1995; he served as chair of APAGS and as a representative to APPIC in 1997. He is currently the chair of the APA ad hoc Committee on Early Career Psychologists. Dr. Prinstein is also an editor of *The Portable Mentor: Expert Guide to a Successful Career in Psychology.*

Shane J. Lopez, PhD, received his doctoral degree in counseling psychology in 1998 and joined the counseling psychology faculty at the University of Kansas, where he teaches courses in psychological assessment and educational leadership. His publications include *Positive Psychological Assessment: A Handbook of Models and Measures* (APA, 2003), *Handbook of Positive Psychology,* and *Positive Psychology.* Dr. Lopez also serves as associate editor of the *Journal of Social and Clinical Psychology*. His research foci include examining training quality, evaluating the effectiveness of hope training programs in the schools (under the auspices of the Making Hope Happen Program), and refining a model of and measure of psychological courage.

W. Gregory Keilin, PhD, completed his degree in Counseling Psychology at Colorado State University and his predoctoral internship at the Counseling and Mental Health Center at The University of Texas at Austin. He is currently the internship training director and assistant director at the University of Texas at Austin Counseling and Mental Health Center. He is the vice-chair of the board of directors of the Association of Psychology Postdoctoral and Internship Centers (APPIC). He led the effort to implement the computer-based internship matching program for APPIC. He also currently serves as the APPIC Clearinghouse coordinator, was involved in the development of the APPIC Directory Online, and administers APPIC's e-mail discussion lists. He is continuously working to incorporate students' feedback into decisions and policies related to the application process and the computer match system.